T0207575

A
Thief
in the
Pantry

On **GOD** our *help* in ages past, Our *hope* for years to come; Our *shelter* from the stormy blast And our *Eternal Home*

Artwork by Madeline Eppard

A Thief in the Pantry

A love story through loss,
resolve, grief, faith, and
victory as Alzheimer's strikes

Marvin B. Eppard

WESTBOW
PRESS®
A DIVISION OF THOMAS NELSON
& ZONDERVAN

This book is a work of non-fiction. Unless otherwise noted, the author and the publisher make no explicit guarantees as to the accuracy of the information contained in this book and in some cases, names of people and places have been altered to protect their privacy.

WestBow Press books may be ordered through booksellers or by contacting:

WestBow Press
A Division of Thomas Nelson & Zondervan
1663 Liberty Drive
Bloomington, IN 47403
www.westbowpress.com
844-714-3454

Because of the dynamic nature of the Internet, any web addresses or links contained in this book may have changed since publication and may no longer be valid. The views expressed in this work are solely those of the author and do not necessarily reflect the views of the publisher, and the publisher hereby disclaims any responsibility for them.

Any people depicted in stock imagery provided by Getty Images are models, and such images are being used for illustrative purposes only.
Certain stock imagery © Getty Images.

Cover Design Art Work by Darwin Nelson

Scriptures taken from the Holy Bible, New International Version®, NIV®. Copyright © 1973, 1978, 1984, 2011 by Biblica, Inc.™ Used by permission of Zondervan. All rights reserved worldwide. www.zondervan.com The "NIV" and "New International Version" are trademarks registered in the United States Patent and Trademark Office by Biblica, Inc.®

ISBN: 978-1-6642-0954-1 (sc)
ISBN: 978-1-6642-0955-8 (hc)
ISBN: 978-1-6642-0953-4 (e)

Library of Congress Control Number: 2020920467

Print information available on the last page.

WestBow Press rev. date: 05/27/2021

As the manuscript of this book was being written, I asked several people, whom I highly respect, to be early readers. Here are their brief reviews of

A Thief in the Pantry

A Thief in the Pantry is a touching tribute to an amazing woman of faith, written by a loving husband committed to honoring God and his wife, recounting his care for her as her mind succumbed to the losses brought on by Alzheimer's. The Eppard's story is both heart-warming and heart-rending as it presents the challenge of consistent, thoughtful care for an Alzheimer's patient, while also addressing the gaps in our current approaches in health care facilities. The story is a beautiful picture of love, one for another and God for us, in marriage and in life.

Cheryl Siemers, Ph.D., Soldotna, AK
Former Academic Dean, Alaska Christian College
Assistant Director for Academic Affairs, Kenai Peninsula College

If you are planning to grow older and would appreciate advice on how to get through one of the toughest dilemmas life can throw at you or a loved one, you will appreciate this poignant, true story. It is an absorbing, personal story that deals with aspects of a degenerative disease for which most of us have no advance preparation. Most importantly, the book is rich with infallible resources specifically designed to give us direction and comfort for the struggles ahead.

Jim Maybach, a fellow sojourner who has profited from
Marv's ability to say the important things

Marv and Jan have been role models, encouragers, and spiritual guides for us for more than forty years. Through this book they continue those roles. Marv and Jan's story gives us confidence that with Jesus we can fulfill the pledge we have made to each other to love and care for each other through anything that comes our way. Thank you, Marv, for your faithfulness and thank you, Jan, for your story. Our memories of you both are inspiring.

Errol E. Wilcox, MA and B. Joyce Wilcox, MA
Punta Gorda, FL

Speaking to her for the first time and sensing that life just changed. Promising at the marriage altar to love and cherish her in sickness and in health. Raising four children together. Serving God and his kingdom together. Then the words of the doctor, "This is Alzheimer's;" followed by a journey, which has no GPS as a guide. In this short but poignant account, Marv invites us to walk with him along the road he traveled, loving and cherishing Jan not only in health but through a decade of sickness. I hope you accept his invitation. You will be blessed if you do.

Rev. Dr. Karl G. Wolfe, Plymouth, MN
Former Director of Distance Learning, Fuller Theological Seminary
Professor, Walden University, Graduate School of Social Sciences

In 2005, it was my privilege to work alongside Marv and Jan at Alaska Christian College. During that time, they were colleagues, mentors, and parent figures to me. More recently, it was a special privilege to serve as the chaplain in the memory care unit of the facility where Jan lived during the last nine months of her life. Marv's book is both a biography and an account of human and divine love. It is a story of pain and loss, as well as joy and ultimate victory. While the thief of Alzheimer's robbed Jan of many things, it could not rob her of the ultimate prize of everlasting life because of redemption in Jesus Christ.

Rev. Dale W. Solberg, Cambridge, MN
Chaplain, Christian educator, and librarian

Years ago, Jan was the first to welcome me when I visited the church that is now my church home. I sensed she was the real deal, for she left the sweet fragrance of Jesus in her wake. As I got to know them, I saw Marv and Jan model what Christian marriage looks like. Once, while visiting Jan, we read from Marv's first book. I told her he was planning to write a book about her. He has, and it's a love story. On one level, it's about Marv's love for Jan. On another level, it's a story of how God sustains us and walks with us through all chapters of life. This book will be helpful to all who find a thief in their midst.

Judie Maybach, Red Wing, MN

Also by Marvin B. Eppard

A Heritage Not Forgotten

The Stories of Four Courageous Pioneers and
Their Journeys to Minnesota Territory

In Loving Memory of
Janice Moon Eppard (Oct. 24, 1931 – June 5, 2019)

For
My Sons and Daughters
Janette, Ruth, Paul, and Bob

Honoring
Those who have and are experiencing
the darkness of Alzheimer's

CONTENTS

FOREWORD

I gladly invited Pastor Marv Eppard and his wife Jan to join the team at our new college in Soldotna, AK in the spring of 2003. We had a need for a Biblical Ethics adjunct instructor, and I knew Marv would be a good fit. When the Eppards arrived, Alaska Christian College was in its second year of discipling and educating Native Alaskan students, and for three spring terms, they served our students both inside and outside the classroom. Officially, Jan worked in our library, but she joyfully stepped in to help wherever she was needed. Together, Marv and Jan loved, mentored, encouraged, and prayed for our students and the ministry of the college. Having previously served as the pastor of Nome Covenant Church in Nome, Alaska, they were both particularly well-prepared to serve these amazing and unique native students . . . and did they ever!

Many fond memories of Marv and Jan's hospitality, generosity, and kindness came to my mind as I read this book, penned by the man who lived through the devastating loss of a beloved spouse over ten years. I visited their home during Jan's decline, and while she didn't recognize me, she taught me something very important. She taught me that when our faith is rooted deep in the truth of Scripture it will not fail us even as our mind slips away. Although Jan was no longer able to form sentences or even speak single words, I was amazed that she could sing the great hymns of faith with me.

Marv also reminded me of something crucial in those

final years with Jan. He reminded me that marriage vows have meaning. When Marv said "I do" to Jan at the altar, he REALLY did. And he demonstrated his commitment over sixty-seven years as Jan's husband, relentlessly serving her through the hard times. Marv lived his biblical vows.

Thanks be to God for the life of a woman who profoundly "spilled" Jesus' love on everyone she met. And thanks be to God for the life of a man who has taught us all, through this book, to "spill" Jesus on our spouses from the altar forward, no matter what may befall us in life's journey.

During my final visit with Jan, I sang this chorus with her, "Because He lives, I can face tomorrow; because He lives, all fear is gone. Because I know He holds the future, and life is worth the living, just because He lives." Now she's singing with the angels in her Heavenly Home.

Rev. Dr. Keith J. Hamilton
President, Alaska Christian College, Soldotna, AK

PREFACE

For ten years, while caring for my wife, Janice, I watched a conniving thief called *Alzheimer's* rob her of all memory and dignity. Much of the time, I kept a journal, recording events, conversations, feelings, and prayers. That which was not written down, is indelibly imprinted in my memory. We were on a journey that had a certain destination, Jan's eternal home. I knew we were surrounded by millions of fellow travelers on the same road. Many people whom I encountered along the way told me of a family member, a friend, or a neighbor who was trudging along with us.

Often, I sensed God nudging me to record our journey in a book, offering hope to others who are, or may in the future, walk the same trail. It is my prayer that this book will be an encouragement to those who may experience a visit from that thief, *Alzheimer's*.

Marvin B. Eppard

ACKNOWLEDGMENTS

Above all, I am profoundly grateful to God for the privilege of sixty-seven years of marriage with Janice, a most amazing woman. It was in prayer that I sensed the urgency to write this book telling our story. When the going was hard, Father God gave me the strength to carry on.

To my family, I express my deepest appreciation. My sons, Bob and Paul, my daughters, Janette and Ruth, and their spouses, Sarah, Maren, John, and Dave have been the greatest all through this story. My grandchildren, Ross, Hugh, Nora, Christopher, Jason, Berit, Mikaela, Tate, and Madeline, along with great grandchildren, Natalie, Eli, and Trey, all stand tall in their grandfather's eyes. A special thank you to Granddaughter Madeline, for the artwork on the frontispiece. Thank you, family!

I am greatly indebted to my daughter, Ruth Anderson. As my editor, she diligently worked her way through these chapters giving invaluable suggestions and countless corrections. Her computer monitor was often blurred by tears as she relived the story she wanted to help me tell. This, while working full-time in a demanding position. Without her support and encouragement, this book would not have been completed. Her sister, Janette Benzen, also read portions and gave constant encouragement.

A special thank you to my friend and colleague, Keith Hamilton, for preparing the Foreword. Keith, with tireless endurance, has seen Alaska Christian College grow from a vision in the minds of a few leaders in Alaska to an accredited college offering associate degrees in several fields. Thank you, Keith, for taking time in your busy life during the Covid-19 pandemic to read the early manuscript and write the foreword.

Thank you to my early readers, Cheryl, Jim, Errol, Joyce, Karl, Dale, and Judie, for the reviews you so willingly prepared. Each of you read the manuscript and wrote your response, often speaking of the impact Janice had on your life.

To my sister, Marlys Glover, I offer my sincere appreciation for her support and encouragement. She spurred me on from the very beginning of this project. Though she is only two years older than me, she still affectionately calls me her "little brother" and it makes me proud. Also from my generation, I offer thanks to Janice's brother, Frank Moon, for reading the chapter about Jan's early life in the Moon family and for the suggestions and corrections he offered.

Thank you to my dear friends, Charles and Jeraldine Whitman, with whom we have journeyed since 1984. They were a continual encouragement through our Sunday evening phone conversations. Chuck read the manuscript and Jerry wrote this tribute to her friend Janice: "During some extremely difficult times in my life, Jan prayed with me, was compassionate, caring, loving, and encouraging. When we visited each other's homes, we cooked, laughed, cried, and shared together. Through this book she will bless your life." Thank you, Chuck and Jerry.

Thank you, Corinne Talbott, Tammy Harold, Joyce Wilcox and Teresa Whitson for being a part of this journey. Your friendship with Jan over the years, and the beautiful tributes that you wrote about her, are priceless. You represent many other wonderful friends who supported Jan and me through the hard years.

A special thank you goes to Kelli Leonard for responding to my "Help Wanted" posting at Minnesota State College Southeast. You were an answer to prayer. You walked into our lives at a critical moment and your gentle, consistent care for Jan allowed us to live in our own home for two more years. Kelli, now a nurse, wrote later, "I want you to know that my time with you and Jan continues to inspire me to take on these types of roles working with patients who live with memory loss."

With gratitude, I give credit to Darwin Nelson, a friend of our family, for his professional photos of the author, of Janice, the family group, and for the preparation of older photos for digital presentation. Thank you, Darwin for the awesome drawing you provided for the cover of this book.

Thank you to my friend, Tim Young, for his incredible computer knowledge. On several occasions, Tim accessed my computer remotely and knew exactly where to click the mouse to get me out of trouble.

Thank you to all the doctors, nurses, nurses' aides, care givers, therapists, care center administrators, and everyone else who contributed to Jan's well-being over our ten-year journey. If you sense any criticism in these pages, please know that it seeped in through the pain and frustration I was experiencing watching my lovely lady disappear before my eyes. Please hear the voice of a spouse who spent every day longing for something better for his wife, knowing that she would not be "better" until she was in the care of her heavenly Father.

Twice we experienced the amazing love and care of hospice agencies. Words fail to show the appreciation I have for both hospice teams. My appreciation mounts when I recall the final weeks, and then days and hours, of Jan's life. You skillfully kept Jan comfortable and I continually sensed your reassurance. Your quiet, gentle presence through that time will never be forgotten.

I am greatly indebted to the WestBow Press staff for their professional service as we moved through the steps from the submission of the manuscript to the completed book that you are now holding.

Marvin B. Eppard

INTRODUCTION

This book is like a journey. It is our true story as a couple in our eighties living with the silent thief called Alzheimer's. The path goes through dark valleys, and reaches the heights of God's grace as we grew in love for each other. It stops occasionally to appeal for relief from the heavy burdens and moves on in gratitude for the stamina to endure. It portrays the infinite value of strong family and community relationships. And it looks ahead, longing for an easier path for those who will travel the same road in the future.

Sifted throughout the story of our ten-year journey with Alzheimer's are two additional themes. One is a call to those involved in the in-patient care of people with Alzheimer's to give urgent attention to improvements that could be made to preserve the dignity of people with this degenerative disease. The other is a recurring awareness, that, when we receive the indwelling Spirit of God through faith in Jesus Christ, we have a source of strength, like a cistern of living water that cannot be diminished by dementia. This is cause for continual thanksgiving.

I write these chapters, not because I think Janice and I accomplished something noble or unique. The opposite is the case. I write because thousands, even millions of people just like us are on the same path. In fact, for many, the journey is even more demanding. Please see this as an effort to encourage those who are in the day-to-day demands of caring for loved ones. Most of all, please hear the call of Jesus to the cistern of life-giving water that Alzheimer's cannot steal.

In this book, names of professional caregivers and care facilities have been changed to protect their privacy. The authentic names of family and close friends were used to enhance the reality of the story. I have been careful to inform these people of the use of their names and have done so with permission.

Marvin B. Eppard

Janice M. Eppard

———∞———

Father God,
as we embark on this journey,
we thank you that you have promised
to never leave us nor forsake us.
Please refresh us
as we drink from the cistern
filled with living water that will never run dry.
Amen

CHAPTER 1

The Pantry

It was the summer of 1942. My grandmother had an old push lawn mower that was in constant need of sharpening. It pushed hard and the lawn was huge. At least that's what it seemed like to a twelve-year-old. The lawn always needed mowing on the hottest days. The task started with a mile-and-a-half bike ride to her home in the country. I would go in the morning, partly to catch the cooler part of the day, but mostly to be sure I would be there at dinner time. On the farm, "dinner time" is twelve noon. It was the biggest meal of the day. Even after my grandfather died, and Grandma lived alone, she always observed dinner time. Grandma's home cooking and a fifty-cent piece in my pocket were my rewards for the day.

Grandma Eppard was a tall woman and rather stout. I don't remember that she smiled very much. She wore her hair in a tight bun on the back of her head and her dress and apron reached the floor. She was stern, not the sweet kind of grandma that a young boy would go to for warmth or comfort. In fact, I can't remember that she talked much at all, but I do remember I liked spending time at her house. I felt safe there.

I was especially fascinated by Grandma's pantry. It was the source of everything. Grandma would disappear into her pantry and come out with thick slices of homemade bread, a plate of home-churned butter and best of all, a jar of tasty jam. Sometimes she would find cuts of ham or sausage patties in the pantry, ready for the frying pan on her big cookstove. The stove, stoked with corncobs, made a hot day hotter, but that went unnoticed by a young boy with a lawn-mower's appetite.

Sitting at the dinner table, I could look through the pantry doorway and see the cookie jar, just to the right of the cistern pump. I don't remember the shape or color of the cookie jar, but I have a distinct memory of the cookies. Grandma's molasses cookies were my all-time favorite.

I loved rainy summer days. Rain meant we wouldn't have to bale hay that day. It meant the grass in Grandma's lawn would grow faster and that meant more fifty-cent pieces. Rain also meant my dad had time to take his old green Ford pickup truck to visit Grandma. I loved going with him because it gave me a chance to do some exploring while Dad and Grandma sat at the kitchen table drinking coffee and eating cookies. Cookie in hand, I would venture into Grandma's pantry.

The most prominent memory I have of Grandma's pantry is her cistern pump. On the counter to the right of the pump, stood a tin can, half full of water, ready to prime the pump when needed next. Water from the cistern was not to be wasted. Another pump, on the front porch, was the source of water for drinking, hand washing, and general needs. Water from the cistern pump in Grandma's pantry was soft rainwater. It was reserved for washing clothes, particularly in the winter. Judging from the way Grandma protected it, that water was very special.

Also in Grandma's pantry was a bread drawer; a large drawer lined with tin. It had a sliding cover also made of tin. This was where Grandma put the loaves of bread she made, once they cooled, after coming out of the big cookstove oven. Next to the bread drawer was the flour bin. Again, tin-lined and capable of holding up to twenty pounds of flour. The sugar jar stood next to the cookie jar on the linoleum counter. The distinct odor in the pantry gave away the fact that well cured bacon, sausage, and ham were stored there. As a boy, I didn't pay attention to where she kept things like yeast, soda, spices, and corn meal. But, I do remember that Grandma's pantry was always neat and orderly. Everything had a place, and everything was in its place.

A door in the far left corner of the pantry held a special fascination for me. That door opened to some rickety steps leading to the cellar. Now, the cellar was the most adventurous place for a boy to explore. It was dark, lit only by two small windows high up in the floor joists. The perimeter walls were lined with large field stones carefully placed together to form the foundation of the house. Rough-sawn beams were strategically located on huge oak posts to support the center of the house. Directly across the room from the cellar steps was a large door held tightly shut by a turnbuckle made of oak with a spike through the center. When turned vertical, the door would open, but when horizontal, the door was securely locked. At first glance, I wondered what could be on the other side. Then I remembered the sliver I got in my back side from sliding down the sloping cellar door at the front of the house. That door was another entrance to the cellar from the outside of the house. Grandma kept that door locked at all times, except during fall harvest when the garden produce was carried down the outside steps to be stored for the coming winter.

Grandma's cellar had a musty odor, partly from the dampness and partly from the cheese that was curing there. In the far corner was a pile of wood all cut to length and size for winter use in the parlor stove. There were sprouting potatoes in the potato bin and carrots buried in garden dirt to keep them fresh. Against the wall behind the steps were shelves made of rough-sawn oak lined with colorful quart and pint jars of fruits and vegetables. Yellowish-orange jars of peaches, pale jars of applesauce, bright green jars of peas and beans, burgundy jars of beets, and dark green jars of pickles. Toward fall time, melons, squash, and pumpkins appeared, sitting in rows on wooden platforms like soldiers in formation.

Grandma's pantry and cellar, while mysterious and tempting, were so well kept and orderly that a young boy would never dare disturb anything. He certainly would not stick his finger in the molasses jar or help himself to a cookie without permission. Grandma's pantry, and the cellar beyond, held many good things, each in its proper place ready for use when Grandma needed them.

Grandma's pantry was the nerve center of Grandma's house. It was the storage place of all good things. From her pantry, Grandma could secure everything needed for a wonderful dinner. Her pantry was a safe place for everything necessary for the care of her family. Tasty food was in her pantry. Beautiful cakes and pastries came from her pantry. A variety of odors came from Grandma's pantry; some not so sweet, but when cooked slowly on her stove, produced mouth-watering main dishes for everyday meals. From Grandma's pantry came the rhythmic sound of the old cistern pump drawing the God-given soft water that she used to keep her family clean, healthy, and nourished.

One day, a thief snuck into Grandma's pantry, quiet and unnoticed. This thief was totally invisible. It was neither male nor female. The thief could pass through doors without opening them. You could neither see nor hear the thief. The thief looked around the pantry and silently slipped away.

A few days later, the thief returned to Grandma's cellar. This time it slipped two potatoes under the garden dirt with the carrots. Later, when Grandma went to the cellar to get two carrots she came out with a potato and a carrot, but she didn't know the difference. Carrots had always been under the garden dirt. While a bit confused, Grandma chuckled in embarrassment at the fact that she couldn't tell a potato from a carrot.

A few months later the thief invaded Grandma's pantry again, this time dumping cornmeal into the sugar jar. Grandma always put two spoonfuls of sugar in her coffee, so the mixture of cornmeal and sugar confused her, and she poured her coffee into the stove causing a smelly burst of scorched cornmeal.

The thief was persistent. The next time Grandma went to the cellar for a jar of pickled beets, she found them mixed with applesauce and stashed behind a cord of wood in a dark corner. One day a stick of kindling wood was found wedged between two jars of stewed tomatoes. At first the thief was not as much interested in stealing from Grandma's pantry as it was to muddle things up so Grandma would be confused and disoriented to the point she couldn't distinguish apples from squash, or cucumbers from tomatoes. Trying to hide her confusion, Grandma became crafty, making everyone think she knew the applesauce from the peaches.

The thief was in no hurry, taking weeks, months, and years to continue the relentless muddling, taking from one thing and tangling it with another. The pumpkins no longer stand guard because they no longer look like pumpkins to Grandma. The cellar steps, once descended with ease, now take her to a place only slightly familiar. Grandma becomes anxious. She gets frustrated, distant, and sullen. The thief causes confusion that robs her of knowing where she is. She begins to think her pantry is somewhere in the distant past and begs for someone to take her home to her familiar, beloved pantry. She starts to think there is a place somewhere in that distant past where everything is in order and things are always where they belong. The days and years go by as the thief not only confuses the pantry, but begins to infiltrate other parts of Grandma's life, causing her to slowly forget the members of her family. She tries to make people think she knows who they are, but people who are close to her see through the ruse. It becomes obvious that she needs constant care to keep her safe. She falls, breaks bones, gets infections, and walks haltingly. She gets days and nights confused, sleeping many day-time hours away and wandering about in the night, interrupting the sleep of others.

As time continues to pass, the thief tires of simply mixing things up and starts to steal items from the pantry altogether. When Grandma goes to get a jar of tomatoes, she finds them missing from the shelf. The thief has jumbled everything to the point Grandma doesn't recognize anything. She no longer can find the bacon to fry on her old cookstove. It becomes dangerous for her to kindle a fire because she may put her dishtowel in the firebox and gasoline in the teakettle.

The thief may steal the cookie jar, but thankfully, there is one precious thing in the pantry the thief cannot touch. The pump beneath the window stands secure, pumping living water from the cistern that will never run dry. From that water pours words of hope and promise drawn from the depths of a heart soaked in the love of her Redeemer and cannot be taken away. Familiar hymns still cause her lips to mouth the beloved words of the Savior. Scripture verses, hidden long ago in the depths of her soul, still linger untouched by an intruder. Living water, fresh from something deeper than memory. A whispered prayer that echoes a heart overflowing with thanksgiving and praise. An unfailing, genuine desire to help other people. A longing to love and teach the little children who, she believes, must be just outside the door. Often waking up in the morning ready to go to school to teach the children an important lesson. Eyes wide with excitement to sew a new garment for a child. Often she asks a stranger (now everyone is a stranger to her), "Do you know Jesus?"

Father God,
thank you for Jan.
Thank you that her heart was
filled with love.
Thank you that now she is where
Love never ends.
Amen

CHAPTER 2

Alzheimer's Is Its Name

The thief, though invisible, sneaky, and conniving, has a name. *Alzheimer's* is its name. No one has ever been able to arrest this thief. It enters uninvited and carves a steady path of destruction on the brain and memory. It has terrorized former presidents and crept up on scientists and doctors. It has attacked the rich and the poor, the educated and the illiterate. No one can predict who the next victim will be. Doctors cannot fully diagnose it except to observe its symptoms. Through autopsies, medical experts have found a buildup of plaque and tangles in the communication systems in the human brain as proof of the disease. No conclusive treatment has been discovered, only drugs that may slow the loss of memory. For a disease that is already dreadfully slow, these drugs are of little help.

Thief *Alzheimer's*, conniver that it is, usually preys upon the elderly when they should be free to enjoy their twilight years. Sometimes though, Thief *Alzheimer's* appears earlier, known as "early onset," producing more pronounced symptoms and a slower, longer decline. You don't catch Alzheimer's–it catches you. You can't hide from it, like we did for months to avoid the COVID-19 virus. You can't wash it away. It passes through unopened doors, making it impossible to avoid.

Alzheimer's gets its name from Alois Alzheimer, a German psychiatrist, who through case studies and autopsies discovered the buildup of plaque and tangles in the brain, causing the dreadfully slow breakdown of communication among brain cells and the gradual process of brain deterioration. Dr. Alzheimer first announced his findings in 1906. Research has continued for over a century, with few results in terms of treatment or cure. Alzheimer's is known as a terminal disease with no criteria for predicting its duration. Scientists have observed the disease enough to predict the stages it may take, but with little ability to know how long it will linger in each stage. While the recipient seems to be unaware of what is happening, family and loved ones can only stand by and watch as Thief *Alzheimer's* slowly and methodically steals every memory and ability.

At some point the ability to remember locations is lost. Words become a constant puzzle. Close family and friends become unfamiliar. Balance goes, causing unexpected tumbles and broken bones. As the disease progresses, the victim's legs become weak and unable to carry weight, making walking impossible. Mechanical lifts become necessary because the thief has taken the part of the brain that tells the legs and feet to work. Hands and arms start to shake, causing food to go flying before it reaches the mouth. Every meal requires assistance.

Brushing teeth becomes impossible, bringing about the need for help with all hygiene needs. Messages from the brain telling the sufferer to hold the head up do not reach their destination. Through years of robbery, Alzheimer's relentlessly dictates the deterioration of all functions until the patient is only able to lie in bed or recline in a wheelchair. Loved ones watch helplessly as weeks, months, and years pass while the patient progresses through phase after phase of decline. Only God, Who is never hopeless, can give the strength to not lose hope.

Come journey with me through the story of an amazing woman, who fell victim to Thief *Alzheimer's*. Her name is Janice. She was known by all her friends as Jan. She had an uncanny ability to remember names of new acquaintances. Time after time she would come home from church and recall the names of several visitor families, including the children and their grades in school. She did it with a genuine love for people, without calling attention to herself. Her focus was always on others, and children responded to her immediately. She dearly loved children and was a gifted teacher of young boys and girls. Many parents could echo Jan's friend Julie, who said, "Jan was our daughter's Sunday School teacher. She led Melanie to the Lord. Melanie invited Jesus into her heart on March 31, 1984."

Difficulty recalling names was the first symptom that I noticed. Jan started to struggle to remember the names of new people that she met. At first, I dismissed it. We were getting older and remembering names is one of the first things to go for many people. Yet the change became more pronounced.

When she started to ask me the names of new acquaintances, I realized something was wrong.

One day, when visiting with our pastor, I asked him if he had noticed anything different about Jan lately.

"What do you mean?" he said, his head tipped to one side and puzzlement in his tone.

I waited a bit and responded, "Oh, about her speech, not being sure of herself. Things like that."

Drawing a deep breath, he said, "As a matter of fact, I've been going to ask you about that. One day Jan wanted to ask me something about my wife, but she couldn't say her name. She passed it off with a bit of embarrassment."

A short time later, I mentioned my concern to our son, Paul, in a phone conversation. "Yah," he said, "we've been noticing some things too, Dad. Last month, Mom sent Maren's birthday card to her mother."

I began to notice other changes. Jan became less talkative in general. She held back in group conversations, not contributing as she always had. Then she started to struggle to remember common words. She would say things like, "Please put that in the. . ." unable to remember the word "refrigerator."

At this point I knew we had to prepare for what may lie ahead. I remembered making an inner personal vow in 2004. Jan and I had volunteered at Alaska Christian College. I served as adjunct instructor of the Biblical Ethics class and Jan served in the library. One of the textbooks for my class was, *An Introduction to Biblical Ethics* by Robertson McQuilkin. From a note on the cover of that book, I discovered that Dr.

McQuilkin had resigned from his position as president of Columbia International University to care for his wife, Muriel, who was advancing through the stages of Alzheimer's disease. I listened to the YouTube message he gave to the student body announcing his resignation. I made this private vow that if that ever happened to Jan, I would care for her as long as she lived.

About five years later, I recall many nights lying in bed next to Jan, long after she had fallen asleep, asking God for direction. I would put my hand on her arm and breathe words like, "Janie, (the name I used when I felt closest to her) is this happening to us?" I knew she could not answer that question, but all through our marriage, when major decisions needed to be made, I always discussed them with her because I respected her discernment. Inside, I knew this was one decision I had to make alone. I knew we had to prepare for the future.

It was a cold winter in 2010. The economy was not good. I was thinking we needed to sell the home we had lived in longer than any other in our entire marriage. It was a home we loved. I had a woodworking shop in the basement where I had built many cabinets and pieces of furniture. Tears came to our daughters' eyes when I mentioned the thought of selling the house and closing the shop. This was a heart-wrenching decision.

But God already had a plan. On the edge of town, was a cooperative apartment building that had opened a few years earlier. I recalled driving past that building while it was under construction, thinking, *I wish we could afford to live there.* Just at the right time, we received an invitation to attend a complimentary breakfast at Village Cooperative. We went. Three units were up for sale. Due to the depressed economy the owners were offering substantial discounts, putting them in reach of our budget. On a stormy day in January, our realtor listed our home for sale on her website. A couple, who had been looking for a home in our town, saw it and asked their realtor to put a hold on it for them until the blizzard let up so they could come to make the purchase. We sold our house and moved into a lovely apartment at the end of February 2010. The first evening in our new home, we stood at the patio door, arms around each other, observing a beautiful sunset, giving thanks to our amazing God.

The next fall, I was called to serve as interim pastor of a church in a small city. We had been there several weeks, having become familiar with our surroundings. One day Jan was planning to go to a meeting and wanted the use of the car. She took me to work and headed back home. A few minutes later, my phone rang, and I heard her troubled voice. "Marv, I'm lost, I can't find our townhouse." I could feel the fear in her words. After making sure she was parked safely, I asked her to tell me what she could see. I gave her instructions to go a few blocks, stop again and call me. Doing this several times, we managed to get her home. After that she no longer wanted to drive the car.

At that point I was even more suspicious that Thief *Alzheimer's* was paying our pantry a visit. We returned home from that interim assignment, relieved that we had already sold our home and were settled in our lovely apartment. I started to do some research to find out what our future may hold. I found that this thief had been at work for a long time invisibly preparing for the days when the thief's work would be outwardly obvious. These revealing words were published in a recent article:

> Alzheimer's disease is a type of brain disease, just as coronary artery disease is a type of heart disease. It is also a degenerative disease, meaning that it becomes worse with time. **Alzheimer's disease is thought to begin 20 years or more before symptoms arise**, with changes in the brain that are unnoticeable to the person affected. Only after years of brain changes do individuals experience noticeable symptoms such as memory loss and language problems. Symptoms occur because nerve cells (neurons) in parts of the brain involved in thinking, learning and memory (cognitive function) have been damaged or destroyed. As the disease progresses, neurons in other parts of the brain are damaged or destroyed. Eventually, nerve cells in parts of the brain that enable a person to carry out basic bodily functions, such as walking and swallowing, are affected. Individuals become bed-bound and require around-the-clock care. Alzheimer's disease is ultimately fatal. (Page 5, 2020 Alzheimer's Disease Facts and Figures SPECIAL REPORT On the Front Lines: Primary Care Physicians and Alzheimer's Care in America)

It was hard to imagine that changes in Jan's brain had been happening for 20 years or more before any observable signs started to appear.

From that time on, Thief *Alzheimer's* was an uninvited guest in our home, and I knew it wouldn't leave until Jan's death would bring relief to her and to all who knew and loved her. Thief *Alzheimer's* was beginning an incredibly slow process of stealing from Jan. It was gradually taking her away from her husband, her children, her grandchildren, and her great grandchildren. She could only pretend that she knew them when they came to visit. Sometimes she would ask me, "Do you have a wife?" I would respond, "Yes, I do. You are my wife and I love you." She would tilt her head and look at me blankly. Like the thief in Grandma's pantry, we watched the agonizing process of decline. Helpless, but not without Hope.

Thank you, Father God,
for shoe box beds and corncob fires
in the old cookstove.
Thank you for a daddy who kept vigil,
making sure his tiny twin girls, Janice and Joanne,
were safe and warm on the oven door.
Amen

CHAPTER 3

Shoe Boxes and Corncobs

hilled through from the cold wind and persistent drizzle, Walter Moon pulled into the farmyard with his team and a triple box load of ear corn that he had picked by hand. Thoughts of an evening with a good book in his comfortable chair by the parlor stove had spurred him on as he worked to finish the last row of corn. He had been pushing himself hard the last few days knowing the weather could get nasty as the end of October drew near. Depression prices for his farm products made it hard to keep going. It was already nearing five o'clock, and he still had chores to do. He would toss a few scoops of his load over the fence for the hogs, throw a tarp over the wagon, and head for the barn to do the milking. Several cows had freshened lately so he had calves to feed. The sheep needed hay and water. And he was hungry.

Glancing toward the house, he saw his wife, Ann, trudging across the muddy yard, heavy with child, her shawl pulled tightly around her shoulders. A concerned look clouded her face. *I can't handle one more thing,* he thought. *I'm exhausted.* Looking over his shoulder, he shouted, "What is it, Ann?"

"I think the baby's coming. I need to get to Tracy. Would you go get Grandma to stay with Mary Ann?" she said with urgency.

Walter was stunned, "I thought it wasn't to be until around Thanksgiving time . . ."

"I can't decide when this baby will be born," Ann said firmly. "Please go get your mother. We have to get to Tracy before the baby comes."

Still Walter hesitated, trying to reconcile the sudden change of plans.

With a stomp of her foot, Ann shouted, "Walter, please go!"

"Ok, ok," Walter replied with a heavy sigh. "I'll unhitch the team and head over and get Grandma and have my brother come and do up the chores. How soon do you think . . . ?"

"I think we have some time. I'm having a little pain and, well, I just know it's close," she shrugged, knowing a man wouldn't understand.

Thinking, *There goes my book and warm chair for the evening,* Walter hurriedly watered and fed his horses and jumped in the old car, hoping it would hold together for some fast driving. On the way to his parent's farm, Walter pressed the gas pedal to the floor and felt the old car respond to his urging. He began to worry, wondering if the baby would be okay, coming a month early like this. When he arrived at his parents' home, he ran up onto the porch and shouted as he crashed through the back door, "Ma, the baby's coming. We need you to stay with Mary Ann." Catching his father's eye as he emerged from the parlor, he called, "Pa, have the boys go out and milk my cows. They know what to do. Come on, Ma, we need to hurry."

Quickly, Grandma pushed the stew she was making for supper to the back of the stove to stay warm, threw a wrap around her shoulders, and followed Walter to the car. On the way back to the farm, Walter gripped the steering wheel and Grandma held on to the seat with both hands.

Upon arriving at the farm, Grandma ran toward the house, meeting Ann on her way to the car. Stopping briefly, Ann said, "Mary Ann is playing in the living room. There's soup on the stove for supper. I haven't told her anything. Better we wait until we know more."

Walter covered the nine miles to Tracy in record time. Ann sat nervously next to him, too frightened to speak.

The next day, October 24, 1931 in a large house that had been converted into a hospital in Tracy, Minnesota, Janice Mae Moon was born. But the family was in for a surprise.

"Oh my, what have we got here?" the doctor said, "There's another one coming."

"What?" Ann tried to catch her breath. "There are two babies? I'm having twins?"

"You sure are. Give me another good push, Ann. Here it comes. It's another sweet little girl!" Settling the second newborn in Ann's arms, he studied her face. "Do you want me to tell Walter, or do you want to?"

Ann smiled and said, "I think you better tell him before he comes in. You may have to treat him for shock."

Janice's twin sister was named Joanne Emma. Jan weighed in at three pounds, eleven ounces and her sister at three pounds, two ounces. Walter and Ann placed the girls in shoe boxes and put them on the oven door of the old cookstove for warmth during their first winter.

Another story could be told about how Joanne became a registered nurse and served in various hospitals around the country, ending her career as an industrial nurse with the Nabisco Company. Interestingly, she died eight days before Jan, having experienced dementia in her final months.

Jan grew up in a very close family. Walter was an amazing man. Born in 1902, he was fourth of thirteen brothers and sisters. Though he loved to read and learn, he left school after tenth or eleventh grade. When Jan wrote her life story for the memory boxes we gave to our children, she said,

> Millard, an older brother, decided to "seek his fortune" in the West, and Walter joined him. Working on wheat farms and in orchards, they finally reached the Pacific where they were hired to work on ships. An old "sea chest" at our farm home when I was growing up was a source of curiosity. It was kept locked, but occasionally my father would get the key out and unlock it when we six children were not around. He would look through his treasures, which he collected

in Hong Kong, Japan, Hawaii, the Philippines,
Alaska and other places during his sailing days
of the 1920's. (From Jan's Life Story)

When Walter was thirteen years old, his family moved from
Iowa to a farm close to Amiret, Minnesota. His parents became
friends with Andrew Clay and his daughters, Ann and Alma.
The two families socialized at church and community events.
Walter and Ann became acquainted and Walter started to show
Ann some attention. They courted for a while before he and his
brother left on their adventures out west. He told Ann that he
would write to her while he was gone.

During his travels around the Pacific Ocean, Walter sent
Ann sheet music of the popular love songs of their day. I was
mesmerized when I could get him into a conversation about his
travels. It must have been a shock to come home, get married,
have a family, and become a farmer on eighty acres.

I admired the man who became my father-in-law. He was a
speed reader who would bring five or six books home from the
library and read one or two of them before going to bed that
night. He told me that when he read a newspaper, he saw six
lines at a glance. Walter was stern in discipline but not harsh.
He expected everyone in the family to do their share to make
ends meet. Early in their lives, he saw that his sons became
skilled at farm chores, including animal care.

Ann, Jan's mother, was the daughter of Swedish immigrants,
Andrew and Emma Clay. Here are Jan's own words from her
life story:

Andrew became an American citizen on June 6, 1899. Andrew and Emma's marriage was on October 16, 1901 at Amiret . . . To their union were born three children: Alma in 1902, Anna in 1904, and Henry in 1906. Emma contracted tuberculosis and died in 1907. The son, Henry, died a year later. Andrew continued living on the farm until his death in 1929. Paternal Grandmother Mary Johnson, Aunt Hulda, and hired girls from the area helped care for the young girls. They attended grade school in Amiret. With no school bus service to Tracy, Anna lived with friends of her father and worked for her room and board while attending Tracy High School. Following her graduation, she went to Mankato to attend the Business College. While there she became ill and eventually had surgery in Minneapolis where one of her kidneys was removed. Returning home, she recovered and then cared for her father who was having health problems. (From Jan's Life Story)

Think of Ann's losses: her mother when she was three years old, her younger brother when she was four, and her father, after caring for him during his final years, when she was a young woman. On top of all of that, she had a kidney removed when she was an older teenager.

Familiar with loss, Ann emerged to be a loving and caring mother and homemaker. She made do with what she had and made everything stretch to the maximum in those depression years. Every year, with the help of her children, she planted and cultivated a large garden. At harvest time she would can many pints and quarts of fruits and vegetables to provide for the long Minnesota winters. When the children were small, she had a "hired girl" part of the time, but very soon, she trained her daughters to be reliable helpers. Ann baked bread regularly for her family. In addition to all of this, Ann saw that she and the children got to church on Sunday where she taught Sunday School and served as pianist for the worship services. One wonders how Ann found the time and energy to be a 4H leader and help each of the children prepare a project for the county fair every year.

Jan grew up doing her full share, not only without complaint, but truly enjoying her surroundings. She learned early to be a giving person and knew the joy of helping. She often told me things about her growing up years with a smile of appreciation. By present standards, the Moon family would be considered poor, but you could never convince Jan of that. They may not have been rich in possessions, but she considered her family to be rich. She grew up wearing coveralls and going barefoot in summer to preserve nicer clothes and shoes for winter. Jan would tell of being excited about a new dress her mother had made from flour and feed sacks that the companies had printed with floral or plaid designs as an incentive for people to buy their product during the Great Depression. Let's go back to those tiny twin girls born to Walter and Ann and placed in shoe boxes on the oven door. Jan can tell the story best in her own words:

My father kept vigil over the fire through the nights during our first cold winter, to be certain we were kept warm in our "shoe-box beds." Early pictures of my sister and me show two skinny little girls, thin blond hair, looking rather malnourished. But, Praise God, we had no serious illnesses, and grew strong, having been blessed ever since with excellent health. Our farm had neither electricity nor running water. A purchase slip dated June 12, 1930, for a one Speed Queen Gas Engine Washer costing $110 was paid off in ten installments. (Previous to this great convenience, the washboard was used.) This was during the depression, but the washing machine was a necessity with our growing family. I remember my mother carrying in snow, melting it on the kitchen stove and doing laundry in the kitchen. Clothes were hung around the house to dry and in the unheated front porch where they froze and were brought in later to thaw and dry. A cistern under the porch gathered rainwater in summer to use for laundry. Kerosene lamps and lanterns provided light in the house and barn. Drinking water was carried in from the pump house, and wastewater was dumped outside. Corncobs were used for the kitchen stove since wood was scarce in our prairie land, and coal was burned in the living room stove, which had isinglass windows through which we could watch the flames burning inside. They showed up well in a darkened room!

Frank Andrew arrived in June of 1934, and a year and a half later, Dwight Henry and Dwayne Virgil were born in November of 1935, barely arriving at the hospital in time because of a blizzard. I remember helping feed them as they sat in their highchairs. My older sister, Mary, a born teacher, had a ready and willing "class" of five siblings to teach. She would proudly go off to the three-room school in Amiret. Then in nice weather after walking home from school, she would become our teacher. The six of us never lacked for someone to play with.

Although life was hard for my parents, we children felt very secure and spent happy hours playing at simple things out in the grove behind the farm buildings, in the barn, in the house, on the stair steps and on the cellar doors. . . My brothers helped our dad with farm work: livestock, milking cows, feeding pigs, etc. . . My outdoors jobs were to bring in corn cobs for the kitchen stove and to gather the eggs. (From Jan's Life Story)

I can still see Jan's bright smile when she would tell of taking care of the chickens on the farm. She would frown when she remembered the sharp beak of an angry "settin hen" fighting to keep her from taking the eggs the hen wanted to incubate. Years after her parents had died and the farm sold, it was a photo of the chicken house that Jan wanted when we drove past the old farmstead. I can still hear Jan say, "We were poor, but we were happy." While Thief *Alzheimer's* was robbing Jan of the last of her memories, I hung an artist's watercolor of the Moon home place on a wall in our home. I knew that was one of the last things she would remember. More than once, a tear ran down my cheek when she pointed to a tiny square far to the left margin of the painting, and whispered, "Chicken house." Jan's life story continues:

> My mother became an adult leader in 4H Club. I learned many homemaking skills and County and State Fairs were opportunities to exhibit clothing, garden vegetables, canning and baking.
>
> When I was in elementary school, my Uncle Ralph and Aunt Ursula Moon with their six children moved to the neighboring farm. My twin cousins, Louise and Lorraine, were the same age as Joanne and me, and we became good friends. The two sets of identical twins often sang together at church and school events.

My mother took us to the Methodist Church in Amiret, where she played the piano, taught Sunday School and worked in the Ladies Aid. I regret that my father didn't participate in our Christian training.

My years of elementary school ended in the spring of 1945 with the Lyon County eighth-grade graduation exercises in Marshall. State Board tests were given in seventh and eighth grades, requiring passing marks to go on to high school. Entering the Tracy School system was a big change from our small Amiret School. Riding the bus, finding our way in the large building, changing classrooms at the buzzers, making new friends, and learning to know different teachers were challenging for us freshmen students. Vocal music became a good outlet of expression for me, and I enjoyed participating in choirs and other small groups. Living nine miles from Tracy made it difficult to participate in after-school activities, but occasionally my father would take us to basketball or football games.

Twin sisters, Janice and Joanne, high school days

When I began dating a classmate in my junior year, I was able to attend more school activities. Eugene was an excellent student and participated in football and basketball. Homecoming of our senior year, my cousin, Louise, and I were among five seniors nominated as queen candidates. Graduation in June of 1949 brought being named to the National Honor Society. I was having a mixture of feelings about being separated from Joanne, who was heading for nurses training in Sioux Falls and I would be at Mankato Teachers College preparing for teaching school.

The day after graduation I left for Frontenac Methodist Camp, near Red Wing, where I worked in the kitchen for the summer. Earlier summers, Joanne and I had worked as "hired girls" for friends of my parents; living in their homes, helping with children and doing housework. Living and working at the camp with young adults gave me a good taste of going away to college. I had never attended youth camp myself, but I enjoyed being in that setting; sharing morning devotions led by the head cook, hearing camp singing, meeting leaders and speakers who came from many communities. (From Jan's Life Story)

From this humble background, Jan ventured into adulthood secure within herself, with a strong faith in God and a vision for her future. She had no way of knowing that years later she would have a visit from Thief *Alzheimer's*.

A mother,
in frustration, slapped her hand to her forehead
and said, "I must be losing my mind."
Her child responded,
"Don't ever lose your heart, Mom,
I'm in there."

CHAPTER 4

Honored and Respected

Wh. hen someone would ask Jan how she came to know and love Jesus, her response would always begin something like this, *"The summer I was nine years old, a team of three young adults led the Vacation Bible School at my hometown church. I loved memorizing Scripture and learning about the Bible, but this was the first time I heard about the need to be born-again. The new experience of having Jesus in my heart was very meaningful to me, though sometimes it was kind of a 'law' thing rather than a relationship with God. I believe God used that time to bring a deeper hunger in my heart for Him."* From that childhood event emerged a quality, Godly woman.

Those Vacation Bible School leaders encouraged her to read her Bible and pray every day. I spent sixty-seven years of days with her and I can vouch for the fact that she did just that almost every day. In fact, after we retired, with more time together, we read through the Bible out loud each year for many years. The stack of spiral notebooks found in the bottom drawer of her desk, along with notes from her Bible studies, attest to her love for God's Word. Our children remember her sitting at the dining room table on Sunday afternoons copying her sermon notes into those notebooks. Not only did she study the Bible, but she lived it. The finish is worn off the surface of her desk from all the letters and cards she wrote. Every birthday, anniversary, confirmation, graduation, illness, death, or just when she thought someone needed encouragement, a card was written. Cards were never sent without a brief loving and encouraging message and she always wrote out an appropriate Scripture verse, not just the reference. She used one of her notebooks to keep a list of verses for special occasions or encouragement during difficult situations.

Jan and Marv with sons, daughters, and spouses

Jan
with son, Paul

Jan with daughter, Janette

Jan with son, Bob

Jan with
daughter, Ruth

Jan was a woman honored by her children. During the years that they watched Thief *Alzheimer's* slowly rob their mother of her memory and her dignity, her children did everything they could to lovingly assist with her care. Their help encouraged me to continue caring for Jan in our home for seven years. At Jan's funeral service, her four children stood before a church full of family and friends, and tearfully shared their love for their mom. In their words:

Janette:
Our mom loved Jesus first of all. There are many words that describe her. These are just a few: Mom was loving, kind, compassionate, giving, selfless, frugal, patient, wise, thankful, and beautiful.

Mom was loving: When we came home for a holiday or family gathering, Mom would leave the things she was doing and greet each of us with a hug, telling us how good it was to see us. She loved her family and had a way of making each of us feel special and loved.

Ruth:
Mom was kind. She always chose to see the good in people and situations. She did not gossip or speak critically of people. Mom had a gift with names–she always wanted to know a person's name–and she remembered it. Children too. And she was so easy to talk to–she could strike

up a conversation with anyone and they went away feeling like she really cared about them and was genuinely interested in them. As she was losing her memory, she sometimes would ask me my name. Then she would say, "I'm glad we had a chance to get acquainted!"

Paul:

Mom was compassionate. I remember the first time I went home for the weekend in my first semester of college. I woke up on Sunday morning, knowing that I had to go back to school that day. I could hear the silverware tinkling in the kitchen as Mom got breakfast ready for us before church. When I walked into the room, she looked at my face and instantly knew exactly how I was feeling. Homesick. A little scared that I'd fail. She didn't say a word. She just hugged me and I knew she understood.

Mom had compassion for the earth, too. She recycled and composted long before it was hip. She loved nature, always pointing out a beautiful bird or flower, even on the Alaskan tundra. She loved to work in her garden, growing beautiful flowers and vegetables that she could share with others.

Janette:

Mom was giving. She put others above herself. She cooked, baked, sewed, and gardened–almost always for the benefit of others. I remember a couple of specific things. . . Dad took a sabbatical and the family moved to CA for three months at the end of my senior year of high school. I stayed behind with family friends to finish the year. Before they left, Mom asked me to pick out fabric and a pattern for a prom dress so she could make it for me. Sometime after they left, a friend invited me to prom. We had a great time, and I'll always remember the dress she made for me.

Paul:

Mom was selfless. Even though she was a wonderful cook, even Mom would sometimes make a mistake. When she did, the food would never go to waste, so when something was burned or crumbled, she'd say, "I'll take that one," leaving the best for the rest of the family.

Bob remembers Mom always being there for us–driving us to practices or rehearsals, attending our games and concerts. Everything we did was so impressive in her eyes. And when something didn't go well, she'd take the burden on herself and say, "I'm so sorry," as if she could feel the pain. And I think she really could.

Janette:

Mom was frugal. When we lived in Lakefield, Mom took apart an old wool coat and made a hooded winter jacket out of it for me. I was about five, and one day I put on my new jacket and walked to a neighbor's house to play. My friend's mother wouldn't let me in because she didn't recognize me and thought I was a boy. I went home crying. Mom called the neighbor, put a pretty scarf on my head, and sent me back over!

Paul:

Mom was patient. Interestingly, Bob especially remembers Mom's patience! Raising the four of us required it! Always the teacher, Mom patiently taught us responsibility. She would give us chores, especially on Saturdays, and we couldn't play or meet with friends until they were finished. Bob and I would iron the cloth napkins and mow the lawn and we'd all clean our rooms. Bob and I always shoveled the snow on our corner lot in Fairmont. Mom would pay us 25 cents, exactly the cost of admission to the indoor swimming pool (and a quiet afternoon at home with us out of the house).

We were free range kids back then. We'd run the neighborhood all day in the summer, but we'd always be home for lunch at noon and dinner at 5:30. Bob says he could hear Mom call for him several blocks away and we were never late.

Ruth:

Mom was wise. I appreciated Mom's wisdom, especially when she gave relationship advice. Never putting down either person. If I complained about something my husband didn't do, she would reply, "Did you ask him to do that?" "Well, no. He should have known to do it." "He can't read your mind, Ruth. Ask him for the things you need."

Janette:

Mom was thankful. Even as dementia robbed Mom of her memory, she would say "thank you." Thank you for what you do for me, thank you for coming, thank you for the meal, thank you. . . I don't know you, but thank you.

Mom was beautiful. Mom was beautiful inside and out. I look at photographs of her as a young woman. Stunning. She's well dressed, most of the time sewing her own garments. But her smile and eyes say it all. She loved Jesus first of all. And she shared His love in her kind, patient, compassionate, genuine, giving, selfless, frugal, wise, thankful, humble, and beautiful way.

Paul:

After all these years, it's so clear that Mom's legacy was to pass all of these lessons on to all of us. We saw it in the tireless care that Ruth and Janette provided her and Dad for so many years. We see it in the meticulous craftsmanship with which Bob does his work at Closets by Design. We see it in the beautiful meals and baking that Janette shares with family and friends. I hear her voice in my head each time we're discussing a new program at school to reach our kids who are struggling. And we see it in the amazing things that her grandchildren and great grandchildren are doing and will do for others. She lives on through all of us. *We love you, Mom. Thank you for loving us.*

At his mom's funeral, Bob stood quietly with his brother and sisters, choosing not to speak. He is a man of few words, but before the service he made the choicest comment of all. I sent a copy of the funeral folder for everyone to proof and make suggestions. One of the questions was regarding the frame for the cover picture, should it be rectangle or oval? Bob immediately wrote back, *"Oval. Mom never had a sharp corner."* That's a priceless tribute from a son about his mom.

Jan was highly regarded by her peers. Without knowing

she was doing it, she mentored many younger women. I asked several of these friends to send me a list of three or four words that came to mind when they thought of Jan. Here are their responses: *loving, welcoming, kind, caring, gracious, hospitality, inviting, blessing, Godly, meek, quiet,* and more. I asked the same women to write some reflections of their memories of Jan.

Her friend Corinne wrote:

> When I think of Jan I think of a gracious homemaker. Her home has always been so warm and inviting, and she knew just how to make people feel welcome. We always knew she cared about us. She modeled hospitality to me. I learned from her that a pot of soup and a warm loaf of bread are the best company food of all. She made it seem easy and that helped me to also take hospitality in stride.
>
> Pastor Marv and Jan came to visit us twice in Mozambique, and Jan ministered to our children and to the other missionary children at our annual conference. Although I'm sure being in Africa was challenging to her, her graciousness was just as evident there. I remember her arriving with a bag of oranges as a hostess gift for me. She knew that I missed fresh fruit, and that was a very welcome gift. She has always been aware of people's needs, large and small. I remember her teaching our

daughter Donna (perhaps in Mozambique) that the secret to good pizza is lots of toppings. She took time with our children and with me. Her questions, for instance, about my parents, also showed her care.

I have been amazed that, in the midst of the fog of dementia, her sweet spirit continued to shine through. Both Pastor Marv and Jan are shining examples of what it means to grow old gracefully, and we are very thankful for them.

When living in Nome, Alaska, Jan and Tammy met together each week for prayer. This is Tammy's response to my request:

> Thank you for the privilege of taking time to remember the ways Jan was so special to me! As I navigate a new season of life, considering Jan's quiet strength, steady grace, overflowing love, and wisdom, I am truly encouraged in profound ways. The memory that comes first when I think of Jan is her telling EVERY single child EVERY single time she interacted with them, "Jesus loves you!" She would intentionally get down to eye-level with a child, look them in the eye, and affirm them with this truth. She was a skilled teacher overflowing with the love of Christ. I learned much from her! We look forward to reminiscing with her one day in heaven. You chose a gem when you asked Jan to marry you,

Marv! I honor you for the care you gave her in this season of your life. Blessings on you.

Joyce, who first met Jan in 1973, responded when I asked her to share ways Jan influenced her life:

> She modeled how to pray the heart of God. Just being around Jan, I felt closer to God. I never saw her angry or frustrated or any other negative state in all the years I knew her. She has always been my idea of the meek and quiet woman I wanted to emulate. Her sweet smile and gentle voice will live in my heart forever.

Joyce's husband, Errol, joined her in saying,

> Marv and Jan, you two have been such a deep and abiding influence in our walk with Father God. You walked with us through some very difficult times. So often we think, 'where are Marv and Jan when we need them!' Father God has used both of you to bless us with your lives, your wisdom, your prayers, and your guidance. You have made an indelible imprint on our lives.

Jan was a Proverbs 31 wife. She supported me tirelessly. I could count on her to keep a positive outlook. She was wise in choosing the right time and words to share constructive criticism, and she always included a helpful suggestion for improvement. She knew and loved God first, then her family, and then the people around her. She, without a doubt, was a quality person. It seems so unfair that she had to spend her last eight years in a continual decline into darkness. Yet, God never promised fairness, but He did promise to be with us always, and that He would be faithful to us. Jan and I learned not to ask God to take Thief *Alzheimer's* from us, but to trust that His presence would be with us through the losses.

Jan was neither a famous actress, nor a gifted athlete. She was not CEO of a major company, nor was she born to royalty. National TV did not announce her death with sound bites of her accomplishments. But she was a woman of humble background who made a mammoth contribution to other people's lives. That is what prepared her to deal with the intrusion of the invisible Thief *Alzheimer's* in her later years. The truths of the Bible and the strong theology of the great hymns reminded us of the deep cistern filled with living water that gave us strength for each day. I can still hear her halting words in prayer and her soft soprano voice in praise of her Savior. That is what sustained us as we experienced loss after loss to the point that death was gain. Many times, we quoted the Apostle Paul, "For to me, to live is Christ and to die is gain" (Philippians 1:21).

I have great respect for the many couples and families who have made this same journey with grace and faithfulness. None of us can know when our doctor may say, "You have cancer," or, "You had a stroke," or any other diagnosis. Neither can we know when our doctor may say, *"This is Alzheimer's."* When I heard those words, I asked, "What do we do now?" Our doctor, who was a good friend and a brother in the faith, shook his head and shrugged his shoulders. That told me that medicine didn't have much to offer.

I am so grateful that Jan and I had sixty-seven years of marriage based on a commitment to the promise, *"To love and to cherish till death do us part."* I know of divorces that have happened because of an inability to adjust to the losses. Also, I observed people in memory care who never even had brief visits from family or friends. Jesus says, *"Come."* He promises to walk with us through whatever our journey may be. I am not suggesting that others should do what we have done. Please know that, regardless of your circumstances, there is a cistern filled with living water for you that will not run dry. My hope is that Jan's story will be an example of what it takes to face hard trials with an inner victory.

O God, please surround those
who live with Alzheimer's and other dementias.
Teach us how to care for them with dignity.
Grant wisdom to those who
awaken each morning with the responsibility
and privilege of caring for Your children
who cannot care for themselves.
May we all drink deeply from the
Living Water that gives us hope.
Amen

CHAPTER 5

It's Not Going Away

According to their 2020 report, the Alzheimer's Association estimates that over 5,000,000 Americans are living in some stage of Alzheimer's disease. They also predict that this number will nearly triple by the year 2050. (2020 Alzheimer's Disease Facts and Figures SPECIAL REPORT On the Front Lines: Primary Care Physicians and Alzheimer's Care in America) That means that over the next thirty years the need for care for people with Alzheimer's will skyrocket. Families will need to find ways to provide home care as much as possible. The cost of care will be far beyond the ability to pay for many families. Public funding for people whose resources have run out will put pressure on county and state budgets. The lack of funding will make it more difficult for care facilities to have the resources to build and maintain buildings, as well as hire and train staff. There are already places in our country where people who need memory care cannot find a facility with available space. A serious problem is looming in the future and significant planning is needed.

As I write these pages, I am sitting in an apartment during a time of "social distancing" to keep myself and others safe from the invisible Covid-19 virus. The administration of my building is urgently following all the regulations provided by our national and state governments. Our government officials are relying upon medical agencies for advice on what we need to do to protect ourselves from that invasive virus. Unlike Covid-19, we cannot hide from or protect each other from the thievery of Alzheimer's. Like in Grandma's pantry, Thief *Alzheimer's* can pass through closed doors. Most likely, Alzheimer's has been robbing people of their memory from the beginning of humankind.

We have come a long way in the treatment of people with mental illnesses. I started my career as a young pastor in southern Minnesota in the mid 1950's. One of my responsibilities was to visit the sick and shut-in members of the church. What a joy it was to listen to their amazing stories and soak up the wisdom of the elders. The tough part was visiting people in the state hospitals. At that time, people who were unmanageable at home or in danger of harming themselves or others were committed to state-provided hospitals. As I write this, I can almost see the rows of patients tied with towels to keep them in their straight armchairs. They lined the hallways and filled what they called the "day rooms." I still recall the odor, a mixture of urine, feces, and vomit. It was often difficult to find the person that a family in the church had asked me to visit. I left knowing the man or woman whom I visited wasn't even aware that I had been there. Sometimes I wondered if I had actually found the one I came to see. Even worse was knowing that some people were locked in small rooms to keep them from harming others. Obviously, some of these people were suffering from various mental illnesses, but I can't help but wonder how many of them were experiencing Alzheimer's.

I recall attending a pastor's conference at a well-known hospital during which we were given the opportunity to observe the administration of electric shock therapy used to treat mental illness. I remember hearing about medical experts who believed that electric shock was the long-awaited break-through for treating the mentally ill. They told us that, in theory, the shock would cause the person to lose all memory, with the idea that good memory would return and bad memory would be blotted out. Electric shock therapy is still used, but much less frequently and more as a last resort for patients with severe depression. Again, I wonder if some of those people were dealing with Alzheimer's disease.

I am thankful for the progress that has been made in the past seventy years. My sincere thanks to the medical community. Thank you, care center administrators. A special thank you to nurses' aides who are in the trenches every day lovingly caring for people like Jan. You work hard to preserve their dignity, all with little recognition. In fact, far too often, people like me criticize your work out of frustration and heartache. In the future, I hope it will be possible to provide you with better training and adequate resources to do your jobs with less stress. We have come a long way, but we still have challenges ahead. The needs are not going away. To that end, we must focus on improving the facilities and methods that will be used to care for people living with the invisible thief called Alzheimer's.

Based on our experience with Jan in Assisted Living Memory Care, I would make a few suggestions to improve the care provided. I would suggest taking a good look at designing new facilities with the rooms or apartments in a circular pattern around the areas for dining, social activities, and nurse's station. This would put every resident in view of the aides and eliminate running up and down long hallways to respond to residents' needs. Another suggestion would be to use better electronic equipment. Monitors in the nurse's station would make it possible to observe each resident at a glance. If laws prohibit this as invasion of privacy, we need to get laws changed. Cell phones with loud ringers are annoying to people with dementia. Also, more space in bathrooms, where much of the care occurs, would be a help to the aides. Track lifts in some rooms would eliminate the need to run after mobile lifts, spending time and energy pushing them up and down the halls.

Since Alzheimer's is a progressive disease, it is also a terminal illness. As a person with Alzheimer's disease moves through the stages of memory loss, they also need progressively different forms of care. Surprisingly, the first care need for many people with Alzheimer's is hospitalization, not to treat the dementia, but to treat conditions brought about by Alzheimer's. I cannot begin to count the conversations I have had with people who spoke of events that led to hospitalization for their loved ones in early stages of Alzheimer's; falls causing broken bones, infections such as pneumonia, or other serious conditions.

During the years that I was Jan's caregiver and advocate, we made three trips to the hospital. The first one happened when Jan collapsed on the bathroom floor and became totally confused. I was sure it was a stroke, but the doctors ruled that out. Jan was in the hospital for ten days, six of which were at St. Mary's hospital, part of the Mayo Clinic complex in Rochester, Minnesota. The symptom was an excessively high temperature every evening. I was extremely frustrated much of the time because the doctors refused to listen to my pleas for them to give attention to her dementia. They were concentrating on finding the infection that was causing the fever and not on the person. Multiple times, they asked Jan to indicate her pain level. Not knowing how to respond, she would look at me for the answer to the question. Then she would indicate a high number. The doctors would increase the pain medication which heightened Jan's anxiety level and caused more confusion. Over and over I pleaded with the doctors, but they paid little attention. I know the doctors were following accepted practices. However, medical personnel need better training on communicating with Alzheimer's patients and their families. The current standards are not working.

Our second trip to the hospital, on New Year's Day 2013, was precipitated by a broken hip caused by a fall. That day, surgeons repaired Jan's hip by installing a metal plate pinning the bone back in place. Three days after the surgery, Jan was transferred to a care center for rehab and therapy. Jan's Alzheimer's was advanced enough that her brain could not send the messages to her legs to walk without help. The third time Jan was admitted to the hospital was for a mild case of pneumonia.

I am not a physician, but I have read most of the materials provided by the Mayo Clinic and many of the recent reports published by the Alzheimer's Association. Here is the conclusion of the Alzheimer's Association's report for 2020:

> Conclusion: This Special Report underscores the urgent need to develop the medical workforce to meet current and future demands for quality diagnosis and care of people living with Alzheimer's or other dementias. Current and projected future shortages in specialist care — geriatricians, neurologists, geriatric psychiatrists and neuropsychologists — place the burden of the vast majority of patient care on PCPs (added: Primary Care Physicians). However, while PCPs recognize that they are on the front lines of this crisis and feel a duty to provide the highest quality care, they report that the medical profession is not prepared to adequately face the problem, acknowledge that there is a shortage of specialists to receive patient referrals, and note that their training opportunities are lacking or difficult to access. The severity of these needs requires solutions that develop the specialty workforce while also improving capacity in primary care.
>
> (Page 71, 2020 Alzheimer's Disease Facts and Figures SPECIAL REPORT On the Front Lines: Primary Care Physicians and Alzheimer's Care in America.)

Home care is a major need for people with Alzheimer's disease. People with Alzheimer's are most comfortable in familiar surroundings with people they knew prior to the disease. Jan may have lost the ability to know I was her husband, but she was always most relaxed when I was with her. The 2020 *Alzheimer's Disease Facts and Figures* report indicates that sixteen million Americans provided 18.6 billion hours of home care valued at $244 billion dollars in 2019. I can't begin to comprehend numbers like that, but I know that I was one of them and so were our children and friends. Some families can provide care for their loved ones at home, others cannot. There is no right answer. Each family needs to figure out what works for their situation.

Last year, many of those sixteen million Americans got up every morning to provide for the needs of a loved one with little or no preparation for the task. Some kind of training, support and encouragement is needed for these stalwart people. The Alzheimer's Association Help Line is a valuable resource, and certainly there are helpful printed and on-line materials, but many caregivers would greatly benefit from even a few hours of *"hands on"* training. Things like dehydration, constipation, incontinence, sundowner syndrome, and certainly others, are foreign to most of us. Someone to talk with about such concerns for a few hours every few months would be a great relief. I had many questions needing answers in a "do it with me" fashion. Yes, I hear the question, *"Who would pay for this?"* I don't know, but if it would help keep people with Alzheimer's and other dementias at home, rather than in care facilities, there should be some money somewhere. We have a major issue on our hands and we need to find innovative ways to deal with it.

The other option is to pay others to provide needed care in the home. Families with ample resources may choose to employ caregivers to provide 24/7 care. This works well when the caregivers are able to blend into the family life. A less expensive option is contracting with caregiving agencies to supplement what the family can provide themselves. I attempted to hire caregiving agencies a couple of times, with disappointing results. High turnover at these agencies means frequently adjusting to a different caregiver, causing anxiety for the Alzheimer's patient and their family.

When home care becomes impossible, the next option is to choose a residential memory care facility to become home for a loved one with Alzheimer's. This is a hard choice that often becomes necessary when the caregiving spouse dies. A large proportion of people living in memory care facilities are widows in their later years. In our mobile culture, families are spread out and unavailable to care for parents needing help, so residential care is necessary.

Improvements in medical care and better nutrition are resulting in greater numbers of older people. Here I sit, at ninety years old, using a marvelous computer in a comfortable apartment, writing these chapters, telling the story of my amazing wife of sixty-seven years and our journey through nine years of her Alzheimer's. It was difficult, but I am abundantly aware of those for whom the journey was much longer and more difficult than ours. Often, when the going was hard and the days got long, I prayed, "O God, please shorten the days."

Pandemics and plagues have come and gone ever since Moses and Pharaoh argued over setting the Hebrews free from slavery in Egypt. I certainly don't believe that God sends viruses or Alzheimer's to plague us. That is not within a biblical view of God. I do believe that God has promised to be with us. He calls us to be faithful, and we can trust Him. If Alzheimer's chooses to pay a visit to you or someone in your family, I pray that God would empower you with His love and grace to meet that need. I'm reminded of the song by Frank E. Graeff, "Does Jesus Care."

> Does Jesus care when my heart is pained
> Too deeply for mirth or song,
> As the burdens press, and the cares distress,
> And the way grows weary and long?
> Oh, yes, He cares, I know He cares,
> His heart is touched with my grief;
> When the days are weary, the long nights dreary,
> I know my Savior cares.

See what great love
the Father has lavished on us
That we should be called children of God!
And that is what we are!

———∞∞∞———

1 John 3:1a

CHAPTER 6

Sweetcorn for Supper?

ld Frontenac Methodist Camp was quiet. The Jr. High campers were in their cabins for a time of rest in the early afternoon. My co-counselor was with our group, so I was free to enjoy the sunny day. Rounding the corner of the camp kitchen, I spotted her sitting on an old wooden chair, a large basket of sweet corn at her feet. As I approached, she looked up with a winsome smile. In her face I saw pure, genuine beauty. My heart jumped as I became aware of her countenance. Years later I would discover that I was observing what Peter called, "The unfading beauty of a gentle and quiet spirit, which is of great worth in God's sight" (1 Peter 3:4).

"Hi," I croaked, trying to find my voice. "Sweetcorn for supper tonight?" She smiled, and I suppose I did too.

"Hi," she responded as she ripped off another handful of husk. "Lots of it."

Our eyes met. She grinned as her head tipped down, but

her eyes stayed behind. An awkward silence followed. Finally I ventured, "I'm Marv Eppard. I'm a counselor this week. It's been great working with Jackson. He's really good with the boys."

"I've gotten to know him this summer, too. I like the way he encourages the kids," she responded.

I waited a bit hoping for a little more information. "Are you from around here?"

"No," she turned and noticed some of her co-workers cooling off in the shade of a huge oak tree behind the kitchen. "I'm Janice Moon. I'm from Amiret." Seeing the puzzled look on my face, she added, "Bet you never heard of it."

"You're right there," I said. "Let me in on the secret."

"It's close to Tracy, in the southwest corner of the state," she answered with a glance toward the other women. I could tell she needed help husking the huge pile of sweetcorn.

"Have you ever heard of Racine? Minnesota that is, not Wisconsin."

"No. Is Racine your hometown?"

"Yes. It's a little town in the southeastern corner of the state, just south of Rochester." I decided to tell her a bit about myself. "I just finished my freshman year at Mankato State Teacher's College and our pastor invited me to help here at camp this week."

She glanced up at me with a surprised look. "I'm going to Mankato State this fall. I want to be an elementary school teacher."

"That's the place to go if teaching is your goal. I'm studying to be an industrial arts teacher and maybe a track coach." I lingered a moment. "Humm, Janice Moon, I'll remember. I'll watch for you this fall." She looked at me as if to say, *Sure, I bet you will.* I realized she wasn't making much progress with the corn. "Sorry for interrupting your corn husking. Could I give you a hand?"

"That's okay, the other girls will help after they get a little break. They just finished washing dishes. Oh, here they come now." She smiled and set her pan down, getting ready to spread out for her helpers.

I could see our conversation was over. As I walked away, I gave her a little salute, "See you at Mankato this fall," I said with a smile.

She smiled back over her shoulder, "Okay," was her only reply.

Jan and friends husking corn at Frontenac Camp

As I walked toward the beach, I knew I would see her again. Looking out across Lake Pepin, a distant train whistle echoed off the Wisconsin bluffs. I was puzzled by the feeling I had inside. *Janice Moon, I will remember you.*

Camp was over the next day. I watched for her, but didn't see her again. I had noticed the class ring hanging around her neck, alerting me that she had a boyfriend back home, and I thought of the girl I had been dating since my junior year of high school.

I returned to my home in southern Minnesota and worked with my dad on the farm for the rest of the summer. Over and over, when driving the tractor in the fields, I would think about Camp Frontenac and Janice Moon. I couldn't draw to mind a mental picture of her, but was aware of the strange feeling of attraction. I knew it was more than her appearance, though she was attractive. Sometimes I felt guilty thinking of her while still spending time with the girl I had been dating since high school. I tried to put these thoughts behind me while I waited for classes to begin at Mankato State.

Back at college that fall I was anxious to see if I would find Janice at the church I had been attending. I hoped I would recognize her if she would happen to be there. I don't remember when I first saw her, but I did find her and we became good friends. The college group at the church planned frequent group activities, and I always made sure there was room in my car for Janice. The class ring was still around her neck, and I was still seeing my high school girlfriend when we were both home on weekends.

Looking back, I know it was important that we were friends before we started dating. Even that early in our lives, God was preparing us for the challenges that were ahead when we reached our eighties. I became increasingly impressed by Jan's character during that year in college. She later told me that she had been praying for a godly husband, and I was the answer to her prayers. At the time, I wasn't sure what godly meant, and I certainly didn't think that word described me. I do know that without the early foundation of respect and love for Janice, I would not have been equipped to care for her through the trial of Alzheimer's many years later. Sound marriages, built on respect, admiration, and God-given love are the ingredients it takes to navigate hard times.

Shortly before the end of the school year, my girlfriend terminated our relationship, and I asked Jan for a date. When I picked her up, the class ring was no longer around her neck. We started building a relationship that led to our marriage the summer after I graduated from college.

In an earlier chapter, Jan told you about growing up on the eighty acre farm in southwestern Minnesota. At the same time, I was growing up on a larger farm in southeastern Minnesota. When I was three years old, my older sisters, Carol and Marlys, and I were devastated by the sudden death of our mother. I hardly remember my mother. I have a vivid mental picture of her lying in her coffin in our house before her funeral. When they took the coffin away, I was engulfed in loneliness. That loss had a profound effect on my life.

A few years after my mother died, her brother died in a car accident, and when I was eight years old, my father married his widow. So my aunt became my stepmother. Her two sons and one daughter became my stepbrothers and stepsister. Two adults, both having lost their first love, married and blended six children, all having lost a parent, into a new family. A few years later, a daughter was born. There were struggles and competitions among the members of my new family, but we actually did as well as could be expected.

Of the bunch, I became known as the "dumb one." It wasn't until I was in college that we discovered that I had severe astigmatism causing great difficulty reading and making classes like English and history very challenging. To compensate, I did well in math and industrial arts. In high school, I would misbehave, preferring the superintendent's office to reading out loud in class. This poor beginning has been a handicap throughout my whole life. Even now, I have to deliberately force my eyes to move ahead over the words on the page.

Doing well in sports gave me an identity. My industrial arts teacher and football coach took me under his wing and encouraged me to become an industrial arts teacher. That is what took me to Mankato State Teacher's College where I met Jan. All along, I know God was preparing us to face the tough times brought on by Alzheimer's in our later years. Jan lost her memory and ability to care for any of her own needs, but she was blessed with a depth of God's love that, like Grandma's cistern, would never run dry.

Jan and I started dating at the very end of my sophomore year of college. After only two or three dates before the school year ended, Jan left to go back to work at Frontenac Camp. I discovered I could get better grades in summer school than the other semesters, so I stayed at Mankato for the summer term. I had an old Ford that often needed encouragement, but I kept it running back and forth to Frontenac nearly every weekend that summer. My respect for Jan grew as I observed the diligence she gave to her work. I also noticed that Jan was highly respected by the other members of the camp staff. Those weekends at the camp turned out to be a wonderful time for us to grow together.

Marv and Jan, dating days

Much of our dating during the next school year centered on the college group at our church. There were several other couples in the group who were dating, and they became our life-long friends. As our relationship grew, I became more aware of Jan's inner beauty. She seemed to be especially comfortable within herself. She wasn't put on or flashy. She was easy to be with, because she was at ease with people. I often would watch her as she related to others. Her attention was on other people rather than drawing attention to herself.

During her second year at Mankato, Janice was selected to be a candidate for homecoming queen on campus. I knew she was a deserving candidate, but the beauty of her character and personality were so much more precious than being a beauty queen. Even before we began dating, I knew she was a quality person, without presumptions. She was genuine to her core. In fact, if anything would have stopped me from entering a dating relationship with Jan, it would have been that I felt I could not measure up to her. Eventually I began to realize that we could grow together into what God had for both of us.

Jan and I were involved in a Bible study at the home of one of the students. I observed the ease with which Jan entered the conversation. Looking back, this is when my longing for God started to grow. It wasn't until my mid-forties that I finally made a true commitment of faith. Jan and I truly were growing together.

No one told me of the tradition of asking a woman's father for the hand of his daughter in marriage. I blundered along until one night, as I was returning Jan to her dorm after a date,

I asked her if she would marry me. She said yes, so I went and bought a ring. On our next evening out, I asked for her hand and put the ring on her finger and gave her a little kiss.

We made plans for me to visit Jan's home on a weekend. Her siblings seemed to be waiting to see if they approved of this guy who was planning to marry their sister. Her mother calmly continued with dinner preparations. Her father came home a bit later. When I entered the kitchen where the family was gathered, Jan's father cleared his throat and said in his deep voice, "I stayed at the pool hall a while. Thought it might be too much of a shock meeting us all at once."

I nervously shook his hand and asked, "Did you win the pool game?" Everyone laughed and the ice was broken. I grew to admire Jan's dad. We didn't discuss matters of faith, but we grew to respect each other.

Jan signed a contract to teach at the elementary school in Worthington, Minnesota the next year and I finished my senior year of college. My summer school effort made it possible to graduate mid-year. Sometime during the first part of that year, I began to sense a call to be a pastor. Along with my studies, I was working nearly full time, including evenings and weekends, at a hardware store. Unable to go to Worthington to see Jan, I called her and said "Jan, I have a question for you."

"Okay, what's your question?" she responded.

"Well," I lingered, "I've been thinking a lot about my future, and I have a lot of questions. I had a talk with our pastor and I told him I've been thinkin' about going into the ministry." It was quiet on the other end of the phone, so I proceeded. "Pastor said I should do my thinkin' on my knees."

Jan chuckled her sweet little chuckle, but didn't speak.

"Well," I went on, "I've been doing what he said, but I'm not sure what's happening." I decided to quit hesitating and come right out and ask my question. "Jan," I began, "If I were to decide to be a pastor, would you still marry me?"

Before I could go any farther, she said firmly, "You are the one I am committed to marry."

"You mean even if I change my plans and decide to go to seminary?" She assured me the engagement was still on. I was elated. This was pre-cell phone days and our allotted three minutes had long expired. We knew we needed some time together. She had a long weekend the next week, so she offered to take the bus to Mankato and stay with her dorm friends. We had a good talk, and I was thrilled that she was willing to support me in our new plans.

Knowing it would be a stretch to make it through seminary with my reading weakness, I applied for admittance to Garrett Evangelical Theological Seminary in Evanston, Illinois. With slightly questionable college grades, I was accepted on probation, giving me a chance to see if I could do the work. I was assigned a faculty counselor. Working with him I was invited to come to the seminary for the spring term to see how it would go. An older student at the house where I was staying took me under his wing and encouraged me. Spending every hour I could in the library studying, I was able to make a B average that term. Jan came to Evanston to visit late in the term and while she was there, she was hired as Children's Librarian at National College of Education starting the beginning of the fall term.

We were married on August 16, 1952 at the little Methodist Church in Amiret, Minnesota. Jan had done a wonderful job planning a beautiful but simple wedding. Our college pastor officiated, and family and friends gathered for the celebration. I was a proud groom and excited about what was ahead of us. After the ceremony and reception, Walter ordered Jan's brothers to wash the decorations off my car while Jan changed to leave on our honeymoon.

Throughout our long engagement, Jan and I were committed to reserve the sexual expression of our love for marriage. Our honeymoon was a time of growing deeper in the oneness God intends for marriage. I am thankful that we were blissfully ignorant of the trials that lay ahead of us. God was already priming the pump that would draw Living Water from the cistern that would not run dry.

A week later we returned from our honeymoon, packed all of our belongings in my old Ford ready to head for Evanston, Illinois. I was unprepared for the tears in Jan's eyes when she hugged her parents and siblings goodbye. I felt some rejection by her sadness while I was chomping at the bit to get out on our own. Later I realized that Jan was leaving a place of security and belonging while I was ready for new adventures.

First Anniversary at seminary

Seminary days were filled with new experiences. Jan loved her job as Children's Librarian at the training school at National College of Education. We were part of a group of seminary couples that met in each other's homes each month. We enjoyed attending concerts at Grant Park and taking trips to museums and other places of interest. We were privileged to hear well-known preachers at various venues in the city. We even made a few trips to Wrigley Field and Comiskey Park. I had my first experience serving on a church staff as a youth pastor. Jan encouraged me when I became discouraged with my studies. Sometimes she woke up early to type a paper that was due that day. I learned how to skim the assigned books and how to write papers in an interesting style that produced good grades. After three years, I graduated, became ordained, and we returned to Minnesota to serve our first church.

During my career, we served in small towns, a three-point circuit, a county seat, and a suburban city. Our last church was in the cross-cultural city of Nome, Alaska. We survived the usual church conflicts and came to know scores of wonderful people. Jan always said, *"I'm not the usual pastor's wife. I don't play the piano, serve as Sunday School Superintendent, or president of the Ladies Aid. I do a lot of things behind the scenes, and I love to teach the children."*

I wish Jan were here to tell about the birth of each of our children and how, at our doctor's advice, we adopted the fourth because Jan always said she wanted four children. After our children were in school, Jan became a teacher's aide. She loved to help struggling children with reading and math. Often in Alaska she was called upon to substitute for teachers in the elementary school. For two years she came full circle to our seminary days, working as assistant librarian at the elementary school in Nome.

For forty years we served churches together. We grew together in our relationship with Jesus as Lord of our lives. We had hard times, and He saw us through. We grew in our love for each other. We learned the joy of forgiving and being forgiven. We didn't have large salaries, but we always had enough. It became a joy to give to causes we came to love. Retirement in the beautiful river city of Red Wing, Minnesota took us back to within fifteen miles of Frontenac, where we first met.

While retired, we were called to serve in interims for churches that were in search of new pastors. Five times we were privileged to respond to that need. Jan quickly fit into those congregations as the encourager she always had been. Missionary agencies invited us to serve in various capacities for short terms in Japan, Mozambique, and Russia. We volunteered for three spring semesters at Alaska Christian College in Soldotna, Alaska in the early 2000's.

All this time, fifty-five years, we enjoyed good health. We were excited about what we were doing and always supported each other. All the while, growing in our love for Jesus and sharing His love with others. We had life-changing experiences as we opened our hearts to the Holy Spirit and we received replenishment from the living waters in the cistern. All along, God was equipping us for the arrival of Alzheimer's in our lives. I am deeply thankful that God gave me a steadfast Christ-follower as my wife.

Marv and Jan
with Tomoko and
Toshi in Japan

Jan with friends in
Provideniya, Russia

Jan and Marv with Dick Page and
Jan's 48 lb. king salmon in Alaska

This Mozambique woman walked miles to bring a gift to Jan

*Therefore, I urge you, brothers and sisters,
in view of God's mercy, to offer your bodies
as a living sacrifice, holy and pleasing to God—
this is your true and proper worship.*

ROMANS 12:1

CHAPTER 7

This Is Alzheimer's

Remember that tiny three pound, eleven ounce baby girl, who, along with her twin sister, was kept warm in a shoe box on the oven door of the old cookstove? Recall, too, how she grew up in a humble but loving family during the "Great Depression" on the southwestern Minnesota prairie. Visualize the attractive young woman who responded with sincere commitment to engagement and marriage with an adventurous young man. Consider the teacher who would get down on one knee and look a pre-school child in the eyes and say with a smile, "Jesus loves you, and so do I." Get in mind the unselfish woman who loved people and found joy in giving far more than getting. Think of the pastor's wife who would rather teach the children about Jesus than have recognition in leadership positions. Now, fast forward with me to the beginning of Jan's decline as Thief *Alzheimer's* took up residency in our home.

During the agonizingly slow process of decline, I went through numerous cycles, fluctuating between commitment and doubt; between contentment and despair. In this chapter, I invite you into our home for a taste of what it is like to care for a loved-one with Alzheimer's disease. I am going to be as candid as possible so you can experience with me the ups and downs of this journey. The truth is, it is a spiritual journey. I would not have made it through the first few months, let alone the next seven years, without the indwelling power of the Holy Spirit.

It was March 26, 2012. I had awakened early, as I often did, to work on the novel I was writing. Sitting at my desk in the den, I heard some commotion and retching sounds coming from Jan's bathroom. Dashing in to help, I found her on the floor, body fluids having released. I turned her to a more comfortable position and grabbed some towels to cover her trembling body.

As I cleaned her up, I said, "I need to call 911 and get some help."

"No, I'm okay," she responded vehemently. "Just help me up."

"I can't get you up alone. I'm afraid I'll hurt you. The paramedics know how to help you and we need to get you to the hospital."

"No," she said firmly, "I can get up by myself." She straightened up and reached for the vanity to pull herself up. I assisted her, pulling the shower bench closer for her to sit on.

While I finished washing her and helping her get dressed, I asked, "Jan, what year were you born, what is your date of birth?" I recalled her confidently responding to that question at every doctor visit with, "10, 24, 31."

She thought a while and said, "2002." I swallowed hard and waited a moment. "Jan, you have two sons, what are their names?" She just shook her head. I was convinced she had

had a stroke. With a sense of urgency, I called 911. Jan was transported to the local hospital in Red Wing, Minnesota.

After four days with a dangerously high fever, she was transferred to St. Mary's Hospital, part of the Mayo Clinic complex, in Rochester, Minnesota. For the next six days, with the help of our family members, I kept vigil with her day and night. My niece provided a hotel room for me across the street. Most nights, when sleep escaped me, I would go and sit with my beloved. Finally, the doctor said, "After all of these examinations and tests, we have not found the cause of Jan's excessively high fever every evening. We are going to arrange home care for you and have you take her home. She'll get better quicker at home than she will here."

Our daughter helped me bring Jan home from the hospital. She went shopping for a bedside commode, shower bench, and many other needed supplies, so I could spend my time with Jan. I knew the hospital stay had increased the cognitive symptoms we had been noticing for more than two years. She had no recollection of the hospital stay, including the ambulance rides. Although a diagnosis had not been officially given, the handwriting was on the wall. It was clear to me that we were facing a long journey. I was deeply thankful for God's promise to not leave us nor forsake us.

I began to research Alzheimer's disease to understand as much as I could about the road ahead. I also wanted to know our options, so I looked into the availability of care facilities in our community. I knew I wanted to care for Jan at home, but I wondered if I had the skills to do that. I found care centers to be expensive. I was glad we were retired and had reasonable retirement income and some savings, yet I knew that if we were to place Jan in care, our resources would diminish quickly. And, I knew Jan would be most content at home.

Learning to care for Jan by myself nearly full-time was frightening. I was thankful for our daughters and sons who gave me wonderful support and help through that transition. For a few weeks, home health care staff made regular visits. A nurse came each week, an aide gave Jan a shower twice a week and therapists came to establish an exercise routine and assistance with general needs, such as getting dressed and hygiene needs. They instructed me in how to assist Jan between their visits. I continued to coach Jan in these activates for months to follow.

While Jan was still able to help in the kitchen, we prepared meals together. Since I had never done any cooking, it was time to learn some simple meal preparation. We enjoyed choosing recipes to make and these became fun times. It was heartbreaking to watch as she slowly lost the ability to do simple tasks, like peeling a potato, or taking the clean silverware out of the dishwasher and putting it in the organizer in the drawer.

One day Jan said, "Today you can make bread."

"What?" I said with surprise. "Spaghetti sauce from a jar, is one thing, but four loaves of bread is something else."

We made bread that day. Jan was still alert enough to give directions and I was able, with her help, to follow along. The bread turned out great. For weeks, we made bread together as I watched her lose her concentration. Then, she started to stay in her rocking chair while I made bread. Perfecting the art of bread-making became an accomplishment that contributed to my well-being. During these months while Jan was able to do some things and was not frustrated by what she was unable to do, we had some good days. We took rides in the country. She was still able to read, but she liked it when I read to her out loud. It seemed like my voice was familiar and soothing for her. We read the Bible together and spent time in prayer. Jan loved music and often asked me to play a CD. I loved it when I could hear her quiet voice singing along, often with her hands lifted in worship.

I wondered when the next shoe would fall. It did, at about 4:00 a.m. on New Year's Day, 2013. I was awakened by a loud thud. Jan had gotten up to go to the bathroom, became confused, and fell on our bedroom floor.

"Jan, do you hurt anywhere?" I asked urgently.

"No," she responded, while I turned her to a more comfortable position. I put some pillows around her and wrapped a blanket over her.

"Jan," I said, "I'm going down to the Commons and get a wheelchair. Don't try to get up. I'll help you as soon as I get back."

I dashed down the hall and found the wheelchair. I blocked our apartment door open and went after Jan. With the chair locked in place, I got down next to her where I could get my arms under her. I took a deep breath, gave a mighty lift, and sat her directly in the chair. Down the elevator we went to our car in the underground garage. Again I picked her up and sat her down in the front seat of the car. I know I would not have been able to do that under any other conditions. To this day, I don't know why I didn't call 911.

It didn't take long to find out that her left hip was broken. We celebrated the New Year with surgery to install a plate and screws to hold her hip in place. Jan spent eighteen days in rehab for physical therapy with a doctor's order not to put more than "toe-touch" weight on her left leg. The therapist constantly reminded her not to step down on that foot. Jan learned to shuffle when she walked with her walker. She never regained the ability to walk without that shuffle.

This brought about another loss, more adjustments, and more grief as I watched my darling wife gradually diminish. By that time, our hearts had been knitted together for sixty-one years. With each loss, my heart fractured a little more. Looking back, I understand now that the hardest part of caring for someone you love with dementia, is the wave after wave of grief that comes as you watch them slowly lose more and more of their abilities. I grieved my losses too—not being able to do things together as we always had, but observing her losses was even more painful.

I remembered the vow I made in 2004 and I reread Dr. Robertson McQuilkin's book, *A Promise Kept*. A battle between earnest resolve to care for Jan for as long as she lived and deep heart-wrenching grief set in. For the next seven years, I felt like a tennis ball being volleyed back and forth between complete commitment and crippling grief. My dear wife was slowly dying right before my eyes, and there was nothing I could do about it.

Since Alzheimer's is a progressive disease, each stage brought another loss. And with each loss, another adjustment. Transitions between stages could take months. For example, one day it appeared that Jan had lost the ability to get up from a chair. The next day she could stand up by herself as always. Uncertainty was my constant companion, often accompanied by expressions of anger. I did not lash out at Jan, but Alzheimer's was my enemy. Unfortunately, sometimes family members bore the brunt of my frustration. "Forgive me" was a much-used phrase as we struggled to support each other through the long months and years.

The Occupational Therapist who worked with Jan after her hip surgery, did some simple testing over a period of several days. With the results in hand, she urged me to take Jan to our primary care doctor. She assured me that he would have the results of her testing. Our daughter accompanied Jan and me to the appointment. In smaller towns, often our doctors are also our friends. Our doctor was not only a friend, but we were members of the same church.

During the general conversation before getting into the examination, the doctor used the word Alzheimer's a couple times. I let it go at first, but as the conversation went on, I said, "Doc, you used the word 'Alzheimer's' earlier. What do you mean by that?"

He looked straight at me and said, "Marv, this is Alzheimer's."

I was taken back when he spoke with such certainty, that I asked, "How can you be sure that Jan has Alzheimer's?"

"I can't be certain," he said. "Actually, the only way we have to diagnose Alzheimer's is through an autopsy. That is obviously too late to make any difference. All I can say is that all of the symptoms are here. I can get you an appointment with a neurologist if you would like to have another opinion."

"What would a neurologist do to make a diagnosis?" I asked.

"A neurologist would order some brain scans and other tests to determine if there is brain damage. Would you like to do that?"

"No, Doc, I've suspected this in my soul for a long time. Now I know for sure. I'm committed to caring for Jan as long as God gives us life. I'll need your help along the way."

Our daughter noticed her mom getting anxious and reached out and touched her arm, "What do you want, Mom?"

Jan looked at the doctor for a moment, and said haltingly, "Is this really bad?"

Very gently and quietly, our doctor talked directly to Jan. "Yes, Jan," he said, "You have Alzheimer's disease. We will all be with you and help you to live with this disability. I will help you, and we have a social worker on our staff who will help you. Your family will help you. You will be well cared for."

As I reached for my jacket, I asked, "Is there any treatment we should start with?"

"The only thing we have is a medication that may slow down the progression. You could try that if you wish," he said. The tone of his voice told me that he doubted the effectiveness of the drug.

We left his office with a prescription, knowing it held little hope. Once again, I renewed my resolve to care for my beautiful wife with all my strength. I realized I loved her more than ever before, and I knew for certain that the one thing I could give her was my love–a deep God-given love that started to grow the day I saw her husking sweet corn. After that doctor visit, Jan would sometimes tell visitors, "Well, the doctor says I have that disease, and I will just have to live with it."

Fortunately, I was greatly blessed by two daughters who took many hours off from their careers and spent thousands of dollars on gasoline to drive thousands of miles to provide me with six or eight hours relief each week from the care of their mother. Alternating weeks, one or the other would arrive either Friday or Saturday morning, often bringing food for the day, to care for their mom. They did it because they wanted to honor their mother by spending time with her as she was slipping away. And, they wanted to support me as I tried to live out the vow I had made.

I was also very fortunate to have two sons, Bob and Paul, who encouraged and supported me in every way possible. They provided gift certificates from restaurants and caterers for meals, relieving me of the stress of food preparation. They supported their sisters, making it possible for them to help their mom. Bob's home was a haven for me when I needed a place to regroup. Paul flew in periodically to have some time with us. Sometimes he came when one of his sisters was with Jan so he and I could spend part of a day together for some guy talk and a good meal out. Bob, Sarah and their daughter, Madeline, came for visits, bringing a pizza and some goodies. Jan loved seeing her grandchildren, even if she didn't remember their names. We definitely worked as a family to see that Jan was cared for.

Jan, being a social person, needed to be with people. I decided it would be wise to be open with our friends about Jan's condition, so I continued to take her to activities and events as long as possible. We went to parties and meetings at Village Cooperative where we lived, and I took her to worship at our church every week. Sometimes it would have been easier to stay home, but our friends and acquaintances were very understanding, and they tried to include her any way they could. A retired nurse who lived in our building said with her beautiful British accent, "Egg custard is comfort food, I'll make some for Jan." About every month or so, six dishes of tasty custard arrived at our door. Other friends brought cookies, soup, chili, hot dishes and more. People in our building invited us to meals in their homes, but gradually that became more and more difficult as Jan began to need help eating.

Sunday became the hardest day of the week. We kept going to worship at our church nearly every week up to the time Jan went into memory care. Throughout her life, Jan had always taken great care with her appearance and I wanted her to look sharp for church. I took her to a hair salon every Friday so her hair would look nice for church on Sunday. It wasn't long before pierced earrings became too difficult for my large fingers, but I always tried to have her wear some kind of jewelry or a colorful scarf. Getting ready to go was definitely a challenge. She often became anxious to "get going" while I was trying to get myself ready as well.

We tried to arrive at church a bit early so we would be able to see friends before the service started. Jan was delighted when high school students stopped to visit with her. Two sisters invited Jan to their school tennis matches at the courts across the street from our home, so I occasionally took Jan in her wheelchair to watch the young players. She would smile and clap for the girls every time they made a score. Young adults, whom Jan had taught when they were preschoolers, now married with children of their own, would bring their babies or toddlers to see "Grandma Jan." She would reach out to pat the child, smile and say, "Oh, my."

Attending worship was important for me as well. In addition to the spiritual nourishment, it kept me in touch with friends and it helped remind our friends of our needs. For a stretch of many months, thirteen couples or individuals from our church took turns having dinner with Jan and me once a week at our home. They would bring the dinner meal, eat with us, and help clean up, often leaving leftovers for another meal. By that time in the progression of Jan's disease, conversation with her was difficult, so the fellowship of those friends was very refreshing to me.

By the time we got home from church each Sunday, we were exhausted. We usually took naps before having lunch. Too tired to cook, I put together a sandwich or another simple snack. Late afternoon and early evening seemed to drag. Sunday evening popcorn was a tradition in Jan's family, so I carried that on. Sundays were hard, but worth every effort.

From March 26, 2012, following Jan's broken hip, until we placed her in memory care on August 24, 2018, I was her primary caregiver. During that 3,049 day span, there were three times that I was away overnight for a combined total of five nights. Two of the three outings occurred because I had reached a crisis point and needed to get away. To make those outings possible, our daughters made arrangements to stay with their mom. An individual with Alzheimer's cannot be left alone for more than a couple of minutes. This is not a complaint. It was my choice to care for Jan. I mention it to illustrate how demanding it is to care for a loved one with Alzheimer's. Families who do not have a person who is willing and able to take on the primary caregiver role are forced to place a loved one in memory care early in the illness.

Each one of those 3,049 days was nearly the same as the one before. We got up somewhere between 7:00 and 9:00 a.m. Thankfully, Jan went to sleep easily at night and generally woke up rested and happy in the morning. Occasionally, she would have vivid dreams and wake up believing they were real. I soon learned not to try to convince her that it was a dream. Rather, I learned to play along with her dreams. Many mornings, after Jan had dreamed about teaching school, I helped her get dressed and ready to go to school because the children would be there waiting. Sometimes dreams were so real to her that I had to discreetly use what is called "therapeutic lying." I would say something like, "We don't have to hurry, Janie. Today is Saturday. There isn't any school today." Usually, she would look sad and say, "Guess I forgot." By the time she was dressed the dream was forgotten.

Toileting, washing, tooth brushing, hair combing, and getting dressed took about an hour. She seldom resisted even when she wasn't sure who I was. I often wondered what I would do if she refused to let me, a man she didn't recognize, help her with those activities of daily living.

Next, it was time for breakfast. She loved applesauce and canned peaches. Nearly every day she ate a dish of canned fruit while I prepared the rest of our breakfast. Toast with jam, a small dish of cereal, and a glass of juice finished off the meal. While at the table, we would read Scripture and a simple devotional. At first, she tried to read out loud, as had been our custom, but soon she became frustrated with the effort and pushed the book away. Losing her ability to read robbed her of a significant pastime. She enjoyed listening to me read to her and we spent many hours that way. The co-operative where we lived had a significant library, so I had a great source of reading material without leaving the building.

By the time breakfast and devotions were done, Jan would begin to show signs of sleepiness, so I would move her to her recliner. I used an old laptop computer, equipped with exterior speakers, to play videos of the familiar hymns she loved. Snuggled under her prayer shawl, Jan would nap for two or three hours every day.

While Jan rested, I would clean up breakfast and get myself ready for the day. I could hear her pleasant voice singing along with the joyful and hopeful words of those old hymns. From the cistern deep within her, came expressions of worship and praise that sustained us from day to day. Having this reserve of hope was priceless. As the disease decreased her functions, her ability to respond decreased, but she never lost the ability to tap her toe in time with the music. On days when I felt particularly discouraged, her countenance and attitude of worship reminded me of God's sustaining care for us. Thanks be to God.

Afternoons were long. When the weather permitted, I took her outside for walks around our building. We would stop to look at the flowers that, for her, were new every day. Pointing, she would struggle to name a flower or its color. A bench on the back side of our building was a perfect place to watch the birds at the feeders, bringing smiles to Jan's face, and giving me a few more minutes away from the confines of our apartment. Cold or rainy weather kept us inside, walking back and forth in the long hallways, sometimes stopping to visit briefly with neighbors.

Supper time was the most difficult time of the day. Being a novice in the kitchen made it a challenge to prepare a meal under the best circumstances. Caring for Jan and preparing a meal at the same time was a juggling act. If I left her in her recliner, she would call to me, interrupting what I was doing. If I brought her into the kitchen in her wheelchair, being a natural servant, she wanted to help, but her diminished ability made that impossible and caused frustration for both of us. Eventually, I solved this problem by doing as much meal preparation as I could during times when she was more content. Sundowners Syndrome, anxiety, and agitation in the late afternoon and early evening, came on a little later in her decline, adding to the difficulty in the evening, especially during the darker months of the year.

Almost every evening after supper, we watched DVDs of hymns by choirs or soloists that Jan loved. Hearing her sing along on "The Lord's Prayer" always brought tears to my eyes. Jan had never wanted to be a soloist, but she loved to sing in a choir or small group. I am so thankful for my memories of hearing her sing her praise to God. I don't know exactly what heaven will be like, but I like to think that Janice is singing with the angels, a wide, bright smile on her face, and her toe tapping the rhythm. She had a cistern filled with Living Water deep inside.

About seven o'clock in the evening, her head would start to nod and she would look toward her bedroom door. Getting pajamas on, toileting and teeth brushing were the final tasks of a typical day. She often pointed toward her bed and asked, "Is that where I will sleep?" Once in her bed, we prayed prayers of thanksgiving to God for giving us strength for the day just past and for His safety through the night.

Emotionally exhausted, I was thankful for a few hours to myself in the evening to watch a baseball game or listen to my favorite Bible teacher on YouTube. In the early months of our journey, I sometimes took a walk outside after Jan was asleep, just to have a few minutes away from the stress and responsibility. Day after day passed with very little variety from the day before. Often I asked myself the question, "Which would I rather be, the person experiencing Alzheimer's or the caregiver?" Purely from the physical standpoint, I was grateful that I was the caregiver because, were the tables turned, it would have been more physically challenging for Jan to care for me.

One evening, after a long, difficult day, I stood with my elbows on the kitchen counter, looking out the window into the night sky. I noticed two vapor trails against the clouds, from jets passing overhead. Memories of numerous flights to Alaska, Mozambique, Japan, and Russia filled my mind, with Jan always at my side, willing and eager to serve others. Then the stark reality hit. I will never fly again. Another loss, another dose of grief. My eyes filled with tears of joy for the privilege of those many trips in the past. I am grateful for all God has given to us together and for the deep cistern of Living Water that sustained us through the long journey.

So Christ himself
gave the apostles, the prophets, the evangelists,
the pastors and teachers,
to equip his people for works of service,
so that the body of Christ may be built up
until we all reach unity in the faith
and in the knowledge of the Son of God
and become mature,
attaining to the whole measure of the fullness
of Christ.

—⊷⊶—

EPHESIANS 4:11-13

CHAPTER 8

The Church in Action

It had been a long night of coughing, headache, chest pain, and generally feeling down. Daylight revealed a gloomy, rainy day. I was glad Ruth was scheduled to arrive for a day with her mom. I tapped her number on my cell phone. She responded with a cheerful, "Hi Dad."

"Hi Ruth. I guess I need your help. I had a bad night. This cough just hangs on. I can hardly get my breath. My head and chest hurt from coughing so hard."

"How can I help, Dad?" her cheerful voice turned to concern.

"I can't think straight. My mind keeps telling me I can't keep taking care of Mom. Could you please stay over for the weekend? I need to get away for a while and see if I can clear my head."

With no hesitation, Ruth responded, "Sure, Dad, I'll be there by 8:30. Maybe you could go up to Bob's for the weekend. You could relax there. Why don't you call him and see if they will be home this weekend."

"That sounds like a good idea," I said. Jan was still sleeping, so I tossed a few things in a duffle bag and took it to the car, ready to leave when Ruth arrived. A frantic feeling came over me. My resolve to care for Jan taunted me while I waited for Ruth to arrive. I wondered if I could care for Jan for another hour, let alone months or years.

"Marv," Jan called, "I need your help." I was a little surprised she remembered my name.

"Yes, Jan, I'm here," I answered as I walked down the hall to the bedroom. "You're a sleepy head this morning. Ruth is coming today to spend some time with you. Let's get you dressed so she can help you with breakfast."

I was startled by the ease with which I greeted Jan while inside I was overwhelmed with the need to get away. I knew I was in a spiritual battle. Deep down I knew Who would win, yet I couldn't wait to leave.

Jan was cooperative as I got her freshened for the day. As we walked toward the kitchen, she was trying to say something, "Do . . . you, am I . . . get breakfast. . ."

"Are you wondering who will get breakfast for Ruth?" I asked. The hostess in Jan was showing through. If a guest was coming, we needed to have food ready.

"Ruth will help you with breakfast," I assured her. "I am going to be gone a while."

Satisfied that Ruth would take care of things, Jan waited at the table for the door to open.

As soon as possible, I kissed Jan goodbye and left, not knowing what I would do or where I would go. I turned left and headed out of town not caring what an officer would do if he observed my speed. A few miles down the highway, I passed the driveway of one of my friends at church. Jim often told me, "Whenever you need a break, come on out and we'll take a walk in the woods. It's a good place to relax."

It was a rainy spring morning, May of 2014, a walk was out of the question, but a visit with a friend would help. Jim saw me making my way to the door across the muddy yard. "Hi, Marv, come on in," he invited. "The fire's going. It's a chilly day. What brings you out this morning?"

I stomped the mud off my shoes as I stepped through the door. "I guess I just need a friend. The load is getting heavy. Our daughter is with Jan and I have a day or two out."

"Glad you felt you could stop in here," he said cheerfully. I was starting to feel better already. "Judie is working today, and I'll be fixing some lunch after a while. Care to join me?"

"Sounds good to me," I answered. "I'm weary and need some rest."

"We've got a guest room in the back part of the house, made to order for a weary traveler. I'll call you when lunch is ready."

"I can't turn that down. It's the very thing I need."

Jim gave me an extra pillow, a glass of juice and a blanket. I stretched out on the bed and soon fell asleep. It took a moment to figure out where I was when I awakened. In that instant, I realized what Jesus meant when He said, "Truly I tell you, anyone who gives you a cup of water in my name because you belong to the Messiah will certainly not lose their reward" (Mark 9:41). I had received a marvelous gift.

"Smells good," I said as I approached the kitchen. "I really slept hard. I had trouble remembering where I was when I woke up."

Jim turned around and with a smile said, "You seemed troubled when you arrived. How is Jan doing?"

"Right now, it seems like she's doing better than I am. It gets long with every day so much the same. She is gradually slipping away. I keep wondering if I can keep on. People are always telling me to take care of myself. One person said the caregiver often dies before the one being cared for. I'm hearing that so often that I'm beginning to believe it."

"I'm sure the load gets heavy sometimes," Jim responded. "You're always welcome here any time you need time out."

After a good talk, and a tasty lunch, I drove away somewhat refreshed, but my mind kept rehearsing, *Marv, you aren't as great as you thought you were. You will never keep that vow. McQuilkin maybe did it, but you aren't McQuilkin.*

Our son, Bob, and his wife Sarah welcomed me to their home that evening. I let them know I needed some quiet time. I was feeling a little better, but my mind continued to be muddled. I went to my room early, tried to read my Bible and pray for new direction. That night, sleep was fitful. Saturday morning came with bright sun and the smell of spring in the air.

Nearby was a walking trail built on an abandoned railroad bed. I started walking down the trail. In the brisk spring brightness, the birds were singing, and my darkness seemed to lift. I called out to God, not caring who heard me. At times I was shouting in frustration and anger. At first, I unloaded my "poor me" feelings. *Of all people, why is this happening to Jan?* I bellowed. *She deserves better than this!* On and on I went with my complaints. *She's one of your most faithful followers. Come on God, You could cure her Alzheimer's if you just spoke the words.*

I came to a crossroad and realized I had been shouting and walking for over a mile. My voice was tired and my body tense. I turned around, done with the shouting and ready to negotiate with God. Soon I realized He would not be changed by my promises. It came to me that I needed to accept His promises. Then He called to my attention what Peter wrote, "Cast all your anxiety on him because he cares for you" (1 Peter 5:7).

Nearly like an audible voice, it came to me that I was not Jan's principle caregiver. God was! He would keep His word. Humbled, I began to sob in confession and contrition. A deep sense of God's love came over me. His love for me strengthened my love for Jan.

That day was a turning point in our journey through Alzheimer's. There were many more difficult days, but I learned an important lesson. I learned that God cares for us more than we can imagine and His perfect love for us makes it possible for us to love others through Him.

That night I slept soundly and awakened with new resolve, ready to go back home and become a co-worker with Father God in the care of my beloved. I was anxious to get on the road to continue our journey.

When I arrived at home, Ruth told me that Jan had coughed severely the previous evening and had slept in the recliner most of the night. Her concern for me was evident on her face. I assured Ruth that I was ready to care for Jan and she could go back to her family.

"You're doing a great job, Dad," she said. "Being here overnight with Mom helps me understand in a small way how hard it must be for you. Keep reading your Bible and stay close to the Lord. With His help, we'll make it." She gave me a hug, threw her backpack over her shoulder, and headed home.

That night, after Jan was asleep, I sat at the kitchen table. As I looked around, I thought about the wonderful place we had to live. Alzheimer's had changed Jan, but she was still the lovely person God gave to me as my wife. *Please God, I prayed, help me to care for her with your love. Love is what she needs most, and who can love her more than me. Please help me love her with the love you have given to us.*

As I was praying, the recurring thought of how the caregiver often dies before the one being cared for went through my mind. *Be sure to take care of yourself.*

"Rubbish," I said out loud, "That thought is from Satan and I resist it. You, Satan, must get out of here. Out of my mind, out of my thoughts, get out of here!"

Startled by my outburst, I realized that negative thinking is one way Satan controls us. James says, "Submit yourselves, then, to God. Resist the devil, and he will flee from you. Come near to God and he will come near you" (James 4:7-8a).

I knew I was under spiritual attack from the enemy, Satan. I also knew God had promised to be with me. I would be reminded of this truth many times in the following years.

I thought back to my involvement in athletics in high school. My coaches never said to me, "Get in the game, Marv, but be sure to take care of yourself. Don't get hurt. Winning players often get hurt more than the losers." No, my coaches would say, "Get in the game, give it 110%. We can win this game. We're a little behind, but we can come back. Let's give it our best." I was learning that God would give me the strength I needed for the days ahead.

I can't say this brought about total victory the rest of our journey, but I often came back to James chapter 4 for assurance. From that time on, when someone would caution me to take care of myself, I would tell them that I resisted that thought. God did not send His Son Jesus to make us losers, but to give us victory over sin and Satan. Trusting Jesus as my Savior requires giving Him my best. Caring for Jan demanded my best. Keeping our eyes fixed on Jesus, we would see her through to the finish line.

That weekend convinced me that it would take a team to care for Jan, honoring and loving her, for the rest of her life. Ruth's willing care for a few days, the rest in Jim's home, and the comfort of Bob and Sarah's home convinced me that victory would come through teamwork. Within the next month, I asked a small group of friends in our church to meet with me to talk about how the church could have a part in caring for Jan. Some rather simple ideas came out of that meeting.

Several couples and individuals volunteered to bring a meal to our home on Monday evenings, giving us some social contact and relieving me from cooking a meal. They helped clean up after supper and often the leftovers provided another meal or two. Some of those friends came multiple times. The response was overwhelming and uplifting.

Jan's friends volunteered to stay with her for a few hours every week so I could attend a men's Bible Study. Teresa was one of the women who came often to spend time with Jan. She knew how to get Jan involved in baking cookies or reading a book. They always prayed together. Teresa shared these words about Jan:

Jan with friend, Teresa

Jan and I had been friends since 2004 when we began walking together almost daily around our neighborhood. We had shared our life stories and spent a lot of time talking (and laughing) about family, daily life, and growing in our faith and relationship with Jesus. A significant foundation of friendship was built over the course of about ten years.

As Jan grew less able to remember me and, of course, my life story, I was still a familiar, friendly face. We continued to engage in conversations about the family she grew up in, the family she raised, and her long marriage with Marv. It was clear from her happy expression and ease of reminiscing that this was a good thing to do together. We plowed the same field of conversation over and over again, rejoicing in our friendship, her history, and our love for Jesus.

Once when I visited, she commented that the cookies someone had brought over had been especially good when they were warm. I began bringing store-made chocolate chip cookie dough for us to make as we visited. We would only make a few each visit. The point wasn't to make cookies. The point was to do something we could delight in together. She could break off the little squares of raw dough and arrange them on the pan. She always reminded me that we needed to save some for Marv.

We made sure to sing when I came over to visit. Jan was in a church choir most of her life, and also played piano, so music that expressed worship and faith was stored deep in her. I am a so-so singer and as we sang, she would occasionally look at me, shocked at what she was hearing come out of my mouth. I would give her an equally shocked expression and we would start to laugh together.

We had had a long habit of praying together when we walked. When Jan could no longer recall specifics about our prayer requests, we began to pray about them more generally. For instance, having been a pastor's wife for so long, she could still grasp the need and significance of praying for the church staff, even if she couldn't remember the details. I read a daily Bible devotional, or a passage from the Bible, and we talked about the depth of God's love and care for us. We talked about heaven and what it would be like to be there with Jesus.

We were fortunate to have served in many ways in the church, which made it natural for people to respond to our need. I am not suggesting that we should serve in order to be served. I am saying that the church is the Body of Christ through which we serve each other. When we are involved in a healthy local church, the Body of Christ, Jesus uses the Body to encourage and bring healing into our lives.

In 2018, when Jan was declining rapidly, I spent some time giving thanks for all the people who had shared in her care. I realized more than ever how important our church had been on our journey. I decided to submit an article to *The Covenant Companion*, our denominational magazine, in which I highlighted how our church had surrounded us with love and care. I prayed it would cause other churches to be alert to the needs of people with Alzheimer's disease. It was published in the January/February 2019 issue and copied here with permission:

Always On My Mind

A PASTOR SHARES THE BITTERSWEET JOURNEY OF CARING
FOR HIS WIFE AS THEY FACE ALZHEIMER'S TOGETHER.

BY MARVIN B. EPPARD | JANUARY 11, 2019

Reality hit me a little more than six years ago when our doctor said, "This is Alzheimer's."

Gentle, caring, faithful, honorable, and generous are all words friends use to describe my wife, Janice. Ten years ago, I began to notice that she was struggling to remember words such as "refrigerator" or "garage." I had to continually remind her to be ready for an event at a given time.

Once she got lost driving in a familiar part of town. Fortunately, she had her phone so I could guide her home a few blocks at a time.

Eventually we had to sell the house we had grown to love over the past fifteen years. It was hard to leave the home that had become the gathering place for family events, but we were able to move to a lovely apartment where I would be able to care for her.

As Janice lost her memory, I lost my wife, my beloved companion and friend. It sent me into a tailspin of compounding grief as the losses mounted.

I confided in friends at First Covenant Church in Red Wing, Minnesota, and they began to plan ways to reach out to us. For many months during this difficult time, thirteen different couples and individuals brought meals and ate with us every Monday evening. Some came multiple times. They gave Janice social contact with people she could still slightly remember. And they gave me much needed conversation, as well as relief from meal preparation.

Every week Janice's friends came to spend an hour or two with her so I could attend a men's prayer group. When I needed new tires on my car, someone from church did the research and took my car to have them installed. Notes of encouragement, phone calls, and text messages—all were signs of support from our church family. Our friends, brothers and sisters in Christ, formed a safety net around us that supported me as I grieved and surrounded Janice with the love she needed.

According to the Alzheimer's Association, Alzheimer's disease is the sixth leading cause of death in the United States and takes the lives of more people each year than breast cancer and prostate cancer combined. More than five and a half million Americans are living with Alzheimer's, and that number is expected to rise to nearly fourteen million by 2050. Additionally, it is estimated that more than sixteen million Americans provided 18.4 billion hours of unpaid care for people with Alzheimer's or other dementias in 2017.

I have become one of those caregivers. Along with the untiring support of our family, and the devoted ministry of our church, we have been able to lovingly care for Janice's needs as the disease progresses.

Before Janice's diagnosis, she and I volunteered at Alaska Christian College during the spring semesters in the early 2000s. As adjunct instructor of biblical ethics, I used the textbook An Introduction to Biblical Ethics, by Robertson McQuilkin, with my students. At that time, McQuilkin announced his resignation as president of Columbia International University so he could care for his wife who was advancing through the stages of Alzheimer's. He said he was doing this because he could care for her with more love than anyone else. As I listened, I knew that if Janice and I experienced anything similar, I would want to care for her—to love her more than anyone else could. Love is what she needs more than anything else.

This is what I have done for the past six and a half years and will continue to do even while Janice is in memory care. In the process, my relationship with Jesus has grown deeper than ever before. I am thankful for God's faithfulness to me and those who share with me in Janice's care.

The great hymns of the church ring clear the message of our mighty God as I play them with Janice every day. She is able to sing along, the words having been implanted in her heart over many faithful years. Even after she lost her ability to find words for conversation, she sings, "Amazing grace, how sweet the sound that saved a wretch like me!" We are constantly reminded of God's faithfulness singing, "O God, our help in ages past, our hope for years to come, our shelter from the stormy blast and our eternal home."

As Janice lost her memory, I lost my wife, my beloved companion and friend.

Last August, at the wise urging of our adult children,

we placed Janice in a memory care unit located near one of them. This was an extremely difficult decision—another series of loss and grieving, including the loss of being near our friends in Red Wing. Within the first month, Janice lost the ability to stand and walk, causing the need for a mechanical lift for transfers. I could no longer get her into her wheelchair alone to take her for a walk, nor could I get her into the car to go for a ride in the country. I have a small apartment nearby, so I can spend quality time with her each day.

After Janice's diagnosis, I learned that Alzheimer's is a terminal disease. There is no cure. The life expectancy of an Alzheimer's patient varies greatly. Depending upon the age at onset, a person can live with the disease from three to twenty or more years. Janice is eighty-seven and in good physical health. I am eighty-eight and in good health. I pray that the Lord will allow Janice to go to her eternal home before I do so I can be there for her until the end.

As Janice has slipped further and further away, I have continued a dreadfully slow process of grieving. Early on, I had times of denial when I would expect her to function as she always had. I have been angry at Alzheimer's for what it has stolen from us. Sometimes I have "poor me" days. The grief goes on and on. Just when I think I have adjusted, I get another bittersweet surprise, like when my wife smiles at me and asks, "Do you have a wife?"

Having served forty-five years as a pastor, I confess that I did not understand the needs of people suffering from dementia. In fact, I can look back and see times that I deliberately avoided such people because I did not know how to relate with them. With gratitude, I recognize that our church has provided ongoing support in tangible and sacrificial ways. I am incredibly thankful. Serving people with Alzheimer's is a difficult ministry for the church because the duration is long and the needs are often hard to communicate.

As the days go by, I am abundantly aware of God's amazing grace and unfailing love. It is my hope that our story may help others reach out to those who need the love and encouragement of Jesus embodied in his people.

(Page 36 *The Covenant Companion* January/February 2019)

When I was a child,
I talked like a child, I thought like a child,
I reasoned like a child.
When I became a man
I put the ways of childhood behind me.
For now we see only a reflection as in a mirror;
then we shall see face to face.
Now I know in part; then I shall know fully,
even as I am fully known.
And now these three remain:
faith, hope and love. But the
greatest of these is
love.

1 Corinthians 13:11-13

CHAPTER 9

Words

aring for Jan with Alzheimer's was a lonely journey. Days turned into weeks, weeks became months, and months became years. It seemed like life was passing me by. Each day was much like the one before, making it hard to keep track of time. We talked with each other, saying the same things over and over. I knew communication was important so I talked with Jan as I helped her each day. In this chapter, I invite you to listen in on some of our conversations. Even though Jan's words became more childish as the days passed, they continued to reveal her gentle spirit.

From the time I first noticed changes in Jan's behavior until the day our doctor said, "This is Alzheimer's," was about five years. The slow progression of the dementia made it impossible to determine an exact starting time. Little things she said or did made me wonder what was ahead. I knew very little about Alzheimer's at that time, so I didn't know what signs to look for. During that five year period, Jan did some cooking. She could care for her own hygiene needs. Early in that period, she was still driving, but she was uneasy about finding her way, and she had two minor fender benders in the garage. Conversation was becoming more limited. We read the Bible together, but she became less willing to read out loud. Then came the broken hip and our doctor's Alzheimer's diagnosis.

After our doctor gave Jan's condition a name in 2013, I began some detailed journaling. These notes reveal the fact that each day looked the same as the day before. Though repetitious, the words we spoke revealed what was happening in our lives together. The next five years, from the doctor's diagnosis to the decision to move Jan into memory care in August of 2018 was a bumpy road, but it was a time of spiritual growth.

Our friends, Al and Judy, who serve in several missions in Soldotna, Alaska, were coming to visit one evening. We had finished our supper and it was nearly time for our visitors to arrive. I said, "Jan, it's such a nice evening, let's go out and wait for Al and Judy on the front patio."

She was eager to go, but I had to make a bathroom stop. I had her sit on a chair by the dining room table. I admonished, "Jan, please wait here, please stay on this chair. I will be back in just a couple minutes. You must wait here!"

Suddenly, I heard a commotion, Jan's groan and the sound of her walker against the door. I rushed to the door and found her on the floor. "Jan, darling, I asked you to wait for me. Are you all right?"

She rolled to one side, looked up at me and said, much like a naughty child, "I was only trying to help."

Those words took all of the parent out of me. No longer was I in the "shame on you" mode. The fall had caused a bit of vomit. I gently wiped her face and, using the gait belt, helped her to her recliner in the living room, ready for our friends to arrive. We had a good visit with Al and Judy. Jan was unusually quiet and withdrawn as I helped her to bed.

Later that night I prayed, *Father God, please help me to remember that Jan is a lovely adult and no matter how childish she becomes, please help me to always treat her as an adult.* A few words had taught me an important lesson.

Jan woke up the next day complaining of pain in her back. Ruth arrived for her regular Friday visit. We took Jan to the emergency room where X-rays revealed another compression fracture in her lower back. The ER doctor prescribed some pain medicine and sent her home. One pain pill caused Jan to sleep most of the rest of the day. Ruth stayed overnight, giving me some much-needed adult conversation.

The next morning, Ruth helped her mother get dressed and ready for the day. Difficulty getting Jan to drink fluids was causing dehydration, which in turn caused issues with constipation. Aware of the need, Ruth urged her mother to give some concerted effort while sitting on the toilet. Jan decided she had been there long enough, looked up at Ruth, and said calmly, "I guess I don't have anything to deposit." One brief comment turned a rather serious morning to laughter.

Some days, Jan was unusually talkative. It seemed like she wanted to entertain me more as a guest than as her husband. One day she asked, "Do you have a mother?"

I answered, "Yes, but my mother died when I was three years old."

"Oh, I'm so sorry to hear that," she said with sincere sympathy.

I asked her, "Do you have a mother?"

"Yes," she said with a puzzled look. "They're all grown up now."

"Do you mean that your children are all grown up now?"

"Yes, my children are grown up," she said with certainty and that ended the conversation.

Red Wing, Minnesota is a beautiful Mississippi River town. In the fall, many visitors are drawn to town to view the multi-colored leaf formations on the bluffs. We were sitting by our patio door enjoying the beauty of the morning when Jan asked, with a confused look on her face, "Don't you have a wife?"

I waited a while before answering. Observing the questioning look in Jan's eyes, I said, "What do you mean, Jan?"

She gave a little shoulder shrug, and said, "Where's your wife?"

I had the feeling she knew, but was asking anyway. I wanted my answer to clearly preserve for her an awareness that we were married. I looked at her for a moment to get her attention and said, "Jan, you are my wife, and I am very proud of you."

She responded, "Oh, yes."

The conversation ended. Similar exchanges like this happened as often as once or twice a day for many months.

Toward evening nearly every day, Jan would ask, "Is this our house?" Without giving me time to answer she would anxiously say, "Will I sleep here tonight? I don't have any clothes with me."

"This is our house, Jan. We'll sleep here tonight. Your clothes are here," I assured.

"Are you going to stay here with me tonight?" she said, looking to me for security. People with Alzheimer's need constant reassurance.

"I feel like I'm in another world," Jan said, feeling disoriented and confused.

"I'm sure you do," I responded. "That's what that disease is doing to you, and we can't stop it. The doctor told us to expect you to be mixed up." I took my Bible and read to her the words we turned to many times when we needed a word from God.

> Therefore we do not lose heart. Though outwardly
> we are wasting away, yet inwardly we are being
> renewed day by day. For our light and momentary
> troubles are achieving for us an eternal glory that
> far outweighs them all. So we fix our eyes not on
> what is seen, but on what is unseen, since what is
> seen is temporary, but what is unseen is eternal.
>
> 2 Corinthians 4:16-18

As autumn slipped into winter, I began to pray for direction in making decisions for Jan's care. I anticipated the loss of walks outdoors and more chance of depression, particularly in the evenings. This is one of the prayers I recorded in my journal:

> *God, I am wondering how we will manage the*
> *winter time. It is easier to feel dark in winter.*
> *Please show me how to care for Jan when she*

senses the darkness of evening. All the time, I have to make decisions. Decisions about meals to fix. Please, Lord, show me the things Jan will like to eat. And, Father, I never know if Jan needs something for pain. She can't tell me, so I need your help. Lord, sometimes I feel overwhelmed by these decisions. Lord, is there someone who could answer my questions? Open my eyes to those around me who could show me the way.

Thank you, God, that I am not alone. Please keep my head clear and my ears open to your words to me. I long to hear your voice. Yes, I hear you say "Come!" Your Word is precious to me, thank you for your Word. Amen

Shortened hours of daylight caused Jan to sleep later in the morning. It also caused her to want to go to bed earlier in the evening. Sleep was our friend all of the years that I cared for Jan. Changes in sleep patterns is one sign of dementia. Some people get mixed up and come wide awake when it is time to go to bed. I constantly gave thanks that Jan slept well and long most nights.

Jan's anxious time of day coincided with my time to prepare supper. In our apartment, the living room and dining room formed one open space. The kitchen was in one corner with large openings to the rest of the area. Jan called to me from her recliner in the living room, "Marv, what are you doing?"

"I'm getting supper ready. Are you hungry? I'm making Tater Tot Hot Dish. How does that sound?"

Ooops, I thought, *that was the wrong thing to say. Giving her options paves the way to a disagreement.* Communication with Jan was almost like learning a new language. It was important to make statements rather than ask questions. Questions confused her, because she didn't know how to answer. When I made statements, she rarely objected.

While the hot dish was baking, I noticed Jan struggling to get out of her recliner. She called to me, "Marv, I can't get up. What are you doing in the kitchen? I want to help."

"I'm fixing our supper. The Tater Tot Hot Dish is in the oven. I'll get the table set and we can read our book for a while." *I think I said that right,* my mind was processing. I hurriedly set the table and read with her for a few minutes. She was wiggly, but she listened as I read.

The oven timer sounded so I closed the book saying, "Supper is ready, let's use your walker and go to the bathroom and wash our hands."

On the way back from the bathroom Jan asked, "Are the children here? Call the children in."

"What children?" I asked. *Oh! Another question,* I thought. *God, help me learn not to ask her questions.*

"The children," she responded as if I were Mr. Stupid himself. "Open that door. They're out there. Let them in."

"Okay, I'll open the door, but I don't think there are any children coming for supper." I got Jan seated at the table and opened the door. She looked down the hall only to shrug it off.

Variations of this conversation happened many, many times. Throughout her life, when supper was ready it was time for the children to come in. I never did figure out what children she was expecting. Was she wanting to invite children from the neighborhood for supper? Or was she back when our children were young and we should call them in for supper? Or was she spanning way back to her farm home wanting to call her brothers in for supper? It really doesn't matter. I do know that was one of the most difficult conversations to deal with.

One day, Jan was certain we had invited guests to our home for the evening meal. She loved to entertain guests and had always done it with grace. She knew how to help guests feel welcome and at ease. She looked at me and said, "Are you the cook here? I don't cook anymore." She thought for a moment, and said, "Oh no, I guess you are part of the family. If you weren't I would offer to pay for the food."

It was exhausting to find the right words to maintain reasonable calm through the afternoon and evening of each day. Once Jan was asleep in the evening, I would come before God and give thanks for my lovely wife, ending the day with a renewed sense of His grace.

Music was a part of every day. Jan was the singer. I tried to hum along. We started to call her walker, and later her wheelchair, her "chariot." Often, when I was transferring her from her recliner to her walker, I would croak out the words by Etta James, "Swing low, sweet chariot." One day, Jan smiled up at me and sang along. Down the hall we went, swinging our shoulders, and guiding the walker ahead of us toward the kitchen. We sang:

Swing low, sweet chariot
Coming for to carry me home,
Swing low, sweet chariot,
Coming for to carry me home.

Joyous laughter broke through the words as we belted out the next stanza,

I looked over Jordan and what did I see
Coming for to carry me home,
A band of angels coming after me
Coming for to carry me home.

With joy surrounding us, I took her in my arms, looked into her eyes, and saw abiding faithfulness and hope. She said so simply, "I love Jesus, do you?"

"I sure do, Janie, and I love you too," I said as I gave her a gentle kiss. She responded with her sweet chuckle. I was reminded of our first kiss on the beach at Frontenac Camp so many years before. Words can be so inadequate.

When the going got hard and monotonous, I would struggle with self-confidence. A mistake or a failure to see Jan's needs would bring on one of my pity parties. In the midst of one of these downers, I said to Jan, "I need to ask you to be patient with me today, I'm having a bad day."

She cocked her head to one side and looked at me saying, "Don't call it a bad day. God made it." A few words brought a quick end to what I thought was a "bad day."

That afternoon, I took Jan for a wheelchair ride on the

paths around the building. She always wanted to visit the flower gardens. I wheeled her up close to one of her favorites. She looked around carefully taking in the beauty. She focused on some little white bell-shaped flowers and said with a bright smile, "Sing . . . angels . . . song . . . sing . . ." I pondered a moment and then remembered the little song,

> White coral bells
> Upon a slender stalk,
> Lilies of the valley deck my garden walk.
> Oh, don't you wish
> That you could hear them ring?
> That will happen only
> When the angels sing.

We started to hum the tune. Joy surrounded us. I gave Jan a little snuggle. She looked up at me and mouthed the word, "Angels . . ." It truly was a day God had made.

One summer evening after supper, Jan called to me from her recliner, "Marv, I need to talk with you."

"Just a minute, Jan, I'm almost done cleaning up the kitchen."

"No," she said urgently, "It's really important!"

Sensing her concern, I swung the dish towel over my shoulder and went to her side. "What is it, Jan?" I asked.

With furrowed brow, she looked at me and asked, "How many children do we have?"

I suggested we name our children. With some prompting,

she was able to name all four. I wondered where this conversation was going.

With a puzzled look on her face, she pondered a while and said, "Maybe we shouldn't have any more children."

Abraham and Sarah flashed through my mind. I said, "I agree, Jan, I think we have enough children. Now is the time for grandchildren and great grandchildren." She put her head back and drew a contented deep breath. Words can be humorous.

One morning we were in the bathroom getting Jan ready for the day ahead. She looked at me and said, "My name is Janice. What is your name?"

I waited a moment and answered, "My name is Marvin."

"Oh," she said, "It's nice to meet you." A lump came up in my throat when I noticed how sincerely she meant what she said.

Later that day I was making plans for our supper menu. I knew how much she liked a certain kind of fish that we bought at the market. Just for something to say that would include her, I remarked, "Jan, we're going to have fish for supper tonight."

Rather than telling me how much she liked fish, she asked cheerfully, "Oh! Did you go fishing?" A thought flashed through my mind, *It sure would be fun to be able to go fishing.* Unexpected words triggered reminders of my losses.

Sometimes we got off to a slow start in the morning. One particular morning, we had been lazy getting finished with our morning schedule. Jan dozed off in her recliner about noon. She slept an hour or so and woke up with a start, saying, "Marv, you need to take me to school for my class."

"Sure," I said, "Let's get you to the bathroom and we'll get ready to go." I wondered what I would do if we ended up in the car with no class for her to attend. A few evenings earlier I had called the Alzheimer's Help Line and asked for some advice with communication techniques. I was advised to go along with Jan's requests while redirecting her as we went. I was willing to give it a try, but anxious about what I would do if it didn't work.

Once Jan was transferred from her chair to the walker, instead of heading toward the bathroom, she went with determination toward the kitchen pantry. She reached in and brought out her apron. With excitement in her eyes, she said thoughtfully, "I guess you will have to take me to my painting class. You know, I don't drive the car anymore."

I needed a delay tactic so I said, "Please sit down on that chair by the door so I can help you get your boots on." She somewhat grudgingly complied, and I took my time getting her boots. In the process, I asked, "Do you know the way to your classroom?" She looked at me as if to say, *Surely you know where my school is!*

I knelt down by her chair, gave her a little squeeze and said, "Jan, I'm so sorry, but I guess that was all a dream." My heart hurt for her.

With sadness in her eyes, she said, "It's okay, I don't have any paints and paint brushes anyway." She looked around and brought up some inner strength to accept things as they were.

With another squeeze, I said, "I'm sorry, that you don't have a painting class to go to."

Jan nodded, and responded, "I never was a very good painter anyway." The sadness slowly drifted away.

She started to stand up. As I assisted her to her walker, I said, "I'm glad it was a pleasant dream. I think you'll get to be a painter in the new heaven and the new earth that we are promised in the Bible. You'll be a really good painter then." She nodded as she settled back in her chair and fell asleep. When she woke up, there was no memory of a painting class. Some words are sad, but also bring joy. I was thankful for the guidance I had received from the Alzheimer's Help Line.

It was about 7:15 on a nice June morning. Jan and I were lying in bed for a few minutes before starting our daily routine. I put my arm around her like I had hundreds of times and said, "I love you so much, Janie."

After a long pause she responded, "I love you, too." I waited until she spoke again. "Do you have any toys to play with?"

"No, I don't have any toys here."

"That's too bad," she replied. Another long delay. Then she asked, "Do you have a daddy?"

"Yes," I answered. "Do you have a daddy?"

She thought a long time and said, "Yes, I have a daddy, but he's not here."

Again, a pause, "Where is your daddy?"

"He had to go to work to get money for food and other things for us."

"Oh, it's good that he has a job. Where does he work?"

"At a big store," she responded quickly.

"You mean Walmart?" I inquired.

With a little chuckle, she said, "No, not Walmart." She waited a long time and then asked, "Do you have a pet, like a dog or a kitty?"

"No, I don't have a pet. Do you have a pet?"

"Yes, I have a kitty, a white one," she said thoughtfully, "with brown spots on it."

"Does your kitty have a name?"

"No, I don't think so. Maybe we could name it Spot."

That seemed to be settled, so Jan asked, "Do you have any friends that come over to play?" Then quite suddenly, she said, "Maybe we should get out of bed so we can have breakfast." She pushed the covers off and tried to get up. She turned to me and said, "I guess you will have to help me get out of bed." I did, with both a lump in my throat and a smile on my face. *She is so precious,* I thought.

Without a doubt, Jan's two most spoken words throughout her memory decline were "thank you." Nearly everything I did to help her produced a sincere "thank you." Many times, I told others, "I am the most thanked person in the world." Jan was a sincerely thankful person. She lived the admonition of the Apostle Paul, "Rejoice always, pray continually, give thanks in all circumstances; for this is God's will for you in Christ Jesus" (1 Thessalonians 5:16-18).

The journey was long and the course was uncertain, but again and again we were reminded by the writer of the Book of Hebrews to fix our eyes on Jesus:

Therefore, since we are surrounded by such a great cloud of witnesses, let us throw off everything that hinders and the sin that so easily entangles. And let us run with perseverance the race marked out for us, fixing our eyes on Jesus, the pioneer and perfecter of faith. For the joy set before him he endured the cross, scorning its shame, and sat down at the right hand of the throne of God. Consider him who endured such opposition from sinners, so that you will not grow weary and lose heart.

Hebrews 12:1-3

Keep
your face to the sunshine
and
you cannot see the
shadow.

———⚬⚬⚬———

HELEN KELLER

CHAPTER 10

Sprains, Shingles and Stones

We were doing well, taking one day at a time. Then one morning Jan started coughing, vomiting, and gasping for breath. I realized this was urgent, so I called 911. The paramedic looked at me with concern on his face, and I nodded. They set out for the hospital with lights flashing. I followed, praying a mixture of prayers. On one hand, I prayed for Jan to get well, if that was the Lord's will. On the other hand, knowing Alzheimer's patients are always susceptible to infections, I prayed if this was the time for Jan to go to her eternal home, that the journey would be peaceful and without pain.

The emergency room doctor ordered X-rays and recommended that she be admitted to the hospital with pneumonia. I returned home to gather a few things so I could spend the next day with Jan. Mid-morning, the doctor on her floor came cheerfully into the room saying, "It's good we don't have pneumonia."

Baffled by the change in diagnosis, I responded, "What do you mean? The ER doctor told me a few hours ago that Jan has pneumonia."

"That happens sometimes. The X-rays may appear to be pneumonia, but when a specialist reads them, the diagnosis is changed to upper respiratory infection. We'll continue the antibiotics, get some respiratory treatments started and she'll be good to go in a day or two."

Two days later, Jan was discharged from the hospital. Four nebulizer treatments were added to our daily routine. The social worker scheduled home visits for the recommended therapy and home care.

The physical therapist, whom I knew to be highly recommended in our community, came for his first session. After guiding Jan down the hall and back, he had her sit down. I saw disappointment in his face when he shook his head and said, "I can't help her. She doesn't have the strength to improve. Without a reasonable expectation for improvement, Jan doesn't qualify for home care following hospitalization," he said.

I felt defeated. I thought, *My strength is fading too.* I blurted out, "What am I going to do? I'm eighty-five years old and my strength is about gone."

"Maybe your doctor would prescribe hospice care," the therapist suggested. "She is pretty weak."

In the process of discharging Jan from the hospital, the doctor had made a comment about hospice care. "She easily could be in her last sixty days," he said rather casually.

All the details were worked out and Jan was admitted to

hospice care on Christmas Eve of 2015. I took a deep breath. A memory flashed to mind. I was on the last lap of a distance race in a high school track meet. "God," I said, "I'm ready to give all I have to make it to the finish line." And that is what we did, only the finish line was much farther away than we expected.

The hospice staff added brightness to our days and took some of the burden off my shoulders. A cheerful and skilled aide came twice a week to give Jan a shower and did extra little things to make Jan feel refreshed and feminine. We continued the prescribed nebulizer treatments and Jan fell back into a familiar routine.

I didn't know exactly what to expect, but being on hospice seemed to mean Jan would decline in the next weeks. The upper respiratory congestion soon cleared up, and Jan seemed to be back to normal. She was doing fine, but I had some surprises to deal with.

Awakened in the early morning with sharp pain shooting up my left leg, all the way to my lower back, caused concern. It subsided and I passed it off as my peripheral neuropathy kicking up a fuss. I had ignored pain in my legs for years, so I went about the days unalarmed. A few weeks passed but the pain was increasing. I finally made a trip to urgent care where I saw a physician's assistant. My cell phone beeped while the PA was asking me some questions. I reached in my pocket and turned it off.

"Do you carry your phone in that pocket all the time?" the PA asked.

It seemed a strange question, but I answered, "Yes, why do you ask?"

"That cell phone is putting pressure on the nerve in your hip causing nerve pain." He responded. "You take that phone out of your pocket and the pain will go away. I've treated truckers with nerve pain who carry a large wallet in their pocket. Moving the wallet to a different location often clears it up."

I wanted to question his judgment, but I had come to him for advice. Back home, instead of decreasing, the pain increased and my leg started to break out in a nasty rash. This time I went to my primary care doctor. He took one look and with one word gave the problem a name, "Shingles." That was not what I wanted to hear.

A beautiful spring day dawned in April. I said, "Jan, today we will get outside for a wheelchair ride." She smiled her agreement and looked toward the coat closet. With a warm jacket around her shoulders and a shawl over her legs, we headed down the hall and out the front door.

As we rounded the corner of the building, Jan pointed with her hand, "Look, dandelions," she said. But the dandelions moved and then fluttered up from the ground turning into a flock of bright yellow goldfinches. Apparently, they had stopped for a rest on their spring migration. Jan laughed and exclaimed, "Beautiful!"

We continued around the building and down a slope near the garage entrance. Suddenly, the wheelchair stopped and momentum caused Jan to lunge forward. To keep her from going down on her face, I pressed down hard on the handles, dropping to my knees on the sidewalk. The front wheels had hit a clear plastic hose left across the sidewalk by the window washing crew. Now, in addition to the pain of shingles, I had sprained the knee on the same leg. The doctor prescribed a knee brace, but it was hard to decide which was more painful, the knee without the brace or the shingles under the brace.

Added to the pain from shingles and a sprained knee, was a nagging throbbing pain in my back. I endured the pain for some weeks, but finally gave in and made another trip to my doctor. X-rays revealed a kidney stone resulting in a referral to an urologist. It took two sessions of same-day surgery to remove the stone. I was wearing down, and I knew it.

The hospice social worker told me about respite care for caregivers. It sounded like the very thing I needed. Jan was placed in a nursing home for several days while I took a break from everyday duties. I followed the advice to relax and let others care for Jan. A day trip to visit my sister was refreshing. It was hard to keep from worrying about Jan, but I was getting some rest, until the phone calls started. Following standard procedure, the nursing care staff called every time Jan fell, even though she was not injured. I became frantic after four or five calls saying Jan had fallen out of bed.

The nurse said, "We get her in bed and tell her to push her call button if she needs help. The next time we make our bed check rounds we find her on the floor." It was evident the nursing home staff was not equipped to care for Alzheimer's patients. We soon realized we had to get Jan out of that place before something tragic happened.

On a family conference call, we decided it was time for Jan and me to move into assisted living. Our son spent a day with me visiting the available facilities in town. By noon, we had materials and prices from most of the possibilities. Over lunch, we made comparisons and surprisingly, the facility we liked best, the one recommended by our social worker, turned out to be less expensive than our second choice. We called to double-check the numbers and were assured they were accurate. Amazed and thankful, we made a deposit to reserve the opening and set a date to meet with the administrator to sign agreements and prepare to move in.

I was feeling relieved as our daughter, Janette, and I went to make final arrangements. A different person was waiting for us with what seemed like a ream of paper necessary to meet all the requirements. "Where's Barb today?" I asked cheerfully.

"She's in training at one of our other facilities today," she responded.

A red flag went up in my mind. The meeting proceeded with one document after another. Then came the rental agreement and care cost sheet. The bottom line was a little over a thousand dollars a month more than what we had been given earlier. I felt heat coming up the back of my eighty-five-year-old financially conservative neck. "That's not what Barb gave us as a bottom line," I blurted. I reached for the notes I had from the earlier conversation.

The administrator said, "Oh, she's new here. She doesn't know about prices."

"Really, if she doesn't know about pricing, why is she allowed to meet with people and give out prices? Do you mean that I am entrusting my wife's care to people who don't even know the price schedule?"

This was not a good start for our move to assisted living. Senior care administrators, please hear some suggestions. Always remember that your clients have spouses, children, and grandchildren who love them and whose hearts are breaking over what is happening to their dear one. Please, always have in mind the care you are offering is more important than the red tape of rental agreements and fees for everything you provide. You advertise with comforting slogans that appeal to weary people. I urge you to make sure that you are what you say you are. Caring for elderly people is a difficult business, but think of how difficult it is to come to the place in life to need what you offer. Bridge the gap between administration and care providers. Show us hearts that care, and it will be much easier for families to give up hard-earned savings to pay for your services.

A few days after moving into our new apartment, we had a conference with the campus nurse. She took Jan's vitals and did the usual things nurses are expected to do. I assumed the questions she asked Jan were to determine the extent of memory loss and to establish care needs. She turned to me and inquired if I had any questions. I had a million, but didn't know where to start. Finally I said, "One of the reasons we are here is to relieve me from some of Jan's care. Will I be able to leave the facility for six or eight hours knowing Jan will be safely cared for?"

"Yes, you must be sure to sign out, so we can contact you in case we need you," she responded.

"How will you know what Jan's needs are in our little apartment down the hall when Jan is there alone?"

She said, "We have sensors in the room that will alert the aides of movement. We will check in on Jan every hour or so to make sure she is safe. She will have her call button to let us know if she needs anything."

I asked, "Will the sensor know that Jan has fallen out of her chair and is on the floor?"

The nurse had to admit the sensor probably would not pick up that movement. I said, "Jan would not understand the call button. She would not remember to push it if she needed something. She was in the nursing home last week and kept falling out of bed. She didn't know what to do with the call button. I would not want the staff relying on a device that she would not be able to use on her own." Jan put her hand out, signaling she wanted us to stop what she perceived to be controversy.

Jan asked the choicest question of all. She asked the nurse, "If I were your mother, would you want her to be here?"

Following a long pause, the nurse answered, "I don't know." The conference ended and I was left with more questions than before.

I don't know the answers, but I do know some of the questions that need to be considered if we are going to be ready to give quality care to the growing number of Alzheimer's and other dementia patients in the future. We must find something between "assisted living" and "long-term care" where severely memory limited people can be safely cared for with the love they so desperately need. I am writing these words on the first anniversary of my beloved Jan's death. It was a dreadfully long journey not only for me, but for our children, and for our friends in our church. We were fortunate to have all the support mechanisms working for us. I strongly urge my readers to make plans for the journey in case Thief *Alzheimer's* visits you. Many, in fact probably most, do not have what we had to meet the needs of a family member with Alzheimer's.

Health care facilities are springing up all over our country anticipating the expanding number of people in their eighties and nineties. I pray that those who are planning and building new facilities will focus on how to best meet the desperate care needs of people rather than the business enterprise. Whatever the motivation, please put people before profit and love before efficiency. Maybe the money spent on beautifully furnished, but little used, lounges and theaters with sloped floors could go into much used living areas where patients can be easily observed by care staff. This is meant to be a fair description of what we experienced and an urgent call for administrators to put priorities on care with an eye to keeping costs as reasonable as possible.

After several months in assisted living, we found that we were not using any of the available care options. My sprained knee, kidney stones and shingles were healed and I was back to caring for Jan much as I had been doing at home. Our daughters continued to alternate spending a day a week with their mom.

Things were not much different than before and we were paying large monthly fees. Realizing we had chosen assisted living too soon, I began to make plans to move back to our cooperative apartment.

All of us had some concerns that my strength would fail. I met with a representative of one of the reputable home care agencies. I listed the things we would need to make it reasonable for me to resume the role of primary caregiver again. I asked, "Can your agency provide these needs?"

"Absolutely," was the answer.

The decision was made to move back to our apartment and the home-care agency started to fulfill their end of the agreement. I knew it would take some time to adjust; however, it wasn't long before the agency wasn't able to provide a consistent schedule with the same staff as I had requested.

One day a new aide arrived in mid-afternoon with responsibility for the evening meal. She started talking before she stepped over the threshold, "Oh! I'm so tired, my first client was at 6:30 this morning, and I've been going ever since. I haven't even had lunch. I am sooo tired!" She didn't stop talking the rest of the day. Jan became nervous and uneasy.

Jan whispered to me behind her hand, "Tell her to leave." We made it through the day, but I knew we needed a different arrangement.

That evening, I prayed urgently for help. I felt like I was on the end of a tree limb that was being sawn off. I was beginning to panic. The safety net that I had expected the agency to provide was slipping away. The care of my wife, whom I admired and loved, was critically important to me. I got down on my knees and cried out to God, *What am I going to do? God, I need help. This arrangement is not working. God, I'm afraid!* I waited a moment. *God*, I said, *I place Jan in your care. How can I be sure she is safe and well cared for?* It was still. I knew God heard me. I expected direction, but not in actual words.

Then, in almost audible words, I heard, "Look close by." Peace came over the room. Unsure what to do, I waited. *God, what do you mean?* It was quiet. I stood up and walked out to the kitchen to my favorite spot to think and meet with the Lord. With elbows on the counter, I looked out into the night sky. *God, what do you mean, 'Look close by?' This is a building where old people live. I can't ask them to help us for the long haul.* Again, I waited. My attention was drawn to the street leading toward town. I lifted my head and saw the lights of the technical school a couple blocks down the street. I spoke out loud, "There's a nursing school over there. Maybe a student would like to work for us, become Jan's friend, help with her care, and do some housekeeping duties." Tears came to my eyes and I lifted my hands in thanksgiving.

The next day, I printed a small "Help Needed" notice, took Jan for a wheelchair ride, and stopped at the technical school. The receptionist smiled, "Someone in our nursing program should like that." We left hopefully.

Two days later, Kelli called in response to my ad, and we scheduled an interview. She walked through the door with a cheerful smile. Our daughters joined the meeting by conference call, and it was quickly evident that Kelli was the answer to our prayers. Kelli became my employee, an encourager, and our good friend. A CPA in our building, and a wonderful brother in Christ, helped me learn how to do unemployment and tax withholding, and for the first time in my life, I was an employer. Best of all, Kelli loved Jan, and could help her with all her needs. Kelli always arrived with a bright attitude that brought a smile to Jan's face. I could leave the apartment while Kelli was there, knowing Jan was safe. Without a doubt, Kelli truly was a gift from God.

Our helper, Kelli

Kelli served us for two years. We attended her graduation and capping ceremony when she received her RN degree. As Kelli transitioned from student to full-time employee, we knew she would not be available to help us any longer. God had that worked out too. Jan had reached the stage in her Alzheimer's where she was having trouble standing and walking. Our daughters were feeling uncomfortable helping their mom transfer. I knew this would lead to placing her in memory care. There is a great need for caregivers with special gifts like Kelli. We were very blessed to have her help for that season in our lives.

"*Don't
call it a bad day,
God made it.*"

———— ✺ ————

JAN EPPARD

CHAPTER 11

Move to Memory Care

Our daughter, Janette, was spending the day with her mother while I had some time out. Colville Park was my favorite place to let down and relax. Often, in addition to the private pleasure boats, huge tows of commercial barges would pass by, propelled by powerful tugboats. And, most fun of all, was seeing one of the Mississippi cruise boats leaving the Red Wing port, accompanied by festive calliope music. When the weather was nice, I enjoyed leisurely walks on the trails along the river.

In winter, the park attracted many eagle watchers outfitted with cameras with long telephoto lenses. I liked spring time best because I could watch the eagles soar on wind currents high above the river. It reminded me of the words of Isaiah:

> Even youths grow tired and weary,
> and young men stumble and fall;
> but those who hope in the LORD

will renew their strength.

They will soar on wings like eagles;

they will run and not grow weary,

they will walk and not be faint.

Isaiah 40:30-31

As I watched the eagles soar, I thought, *If youths grow tired and young men stumble, what about old men with heavy burdens?* Again, I placed my hope in the Lord, and He helped me renew my vow to care for Jan. But I knew she was declining.

My cell phone chirped. Janette's name appeared on the screen. "Hi Janette," I answered. I could hear her breathing, but she didn't speak. "Janette, are you all right?"

She spoke through tears, "Dad, it's time to take Mom to the bathroom, but I can't get her up from her chair. I'm afraid she will fall. She's upset with me. Can you come home?"

"Yes, I'll be there in ten minutes. I'm at the park. Just wait until I get there." We hung up and I dashed toward home. On the route home, I passed the Minnesota Correctional Facility. The main building is old and forbidding. The high chain-link fence with hooked top and barbed wire added to the daunting look of the facility. I thought, *What would it be like to be in there? I feel confined by Jan's needs, but that's nothing compared to a place like that. Lord, I trust you. Please help me to not grow weary.*

At home, Janette was heartbroken. She felt that she had let me down by asking me to come home, knowing how much I needed the relief her visits provided. And, her mom's anger hurt her deeply. By this time, Janette had been making the four-hour round trip to our home every other week for over six years. Janette's love language is gift giving, so she never arrived empty handed. A day or two before a trip, she would bake bread, make a casserole and often a sweet treat to take along. She was determined to help me care for her mom for as long as she lived, but she was growing weary too. I knew we were one step closer to placing Jan in memory care. With Kelli's graduation making her unavailable, and Jan's legs weakening, I began to feel the inevitable had come. We got Jan settled, and Janette felt comfortable enough for me to leave; this time not to the relaxing city park, but to our church to pray.

God, I pleaded, *What am I going to do? You know how much I want to care for Jan as long as she lives. I know I could die before she does. Lord, I can't keep putting the load on my daughters. Thank you for all they have given.* I continued to pray and appeal to God for answers. I'm not sure how long I lingered in the sanctuary of our church. I felt close to God in this special place where I had spent so many hours over the past years. My phone beeped and I glanced at the print-out. "Hello, Delores," I answered. "What's up?"

Delores, the owner and director of Hope Residence responded, "I wanted to let you know that I have a room available for Jan if you are interested."

"Strange you would call just now. We have reached the point where we have to make some changes. Kelli, our helper, has graduated from nursing school and is not available anymore.

It's getting harder for my daughters to help Jan. Tell me what you have in mind."

"I'm at my office now. Would you like to come over?"

"Sure, I'll be there in a few minutes." I gave thanks to God for His constant care, grabbed my things, and headed across town, praying for wisdom.

Delores met me at the door with a smile. "You made that trip in record time," she said as she led me down a short hall to a pleasant room. We talked about options and then she added, "Marv, I've been thinking. Would you be interested in coming here for your meals and helping Jan with hers? I would provide your meals in exchange for helping her. That would keep my aides free to help other residents."

That sounded appealing. "Delores, you have been so kind to keep me on your list for several years now. I want to be open with you as we make this decision. Janette has been looking at facilities in her area. It may be necessary for Jan and me to move closer to her. Would you be willing to hold your offer for a few days while we work this out?"

"Sure. This room needs some cleaning and decorating. I'll hold it for you until the end of the month." I drove back home praising God.

My vow to care for Jan "as long as we both shall live," was heavy on my mind. I was thankful that we had two viable options. Once again, it was decision time. This decision seemed more critical than any.

Back home, Janette had supper ready. As we shared the meal, I told her about my visit to Hope Residence. She smiled with amazement at God's answer to prayer. Janette left that evening having agreed to look more diligently for an opening for Jan near her home. Family conference calls, emails with photos of possible memory care facilities, and much prayer filled the following days.

I wanted to be stubborn and demanding, insisting that Jan and I stay in Red Wing. I could hardly bear the thought of leaving our church and friendships that we had built over twenty-three years. Moving felt like giving up on my vow to care for Jan. I also recalled the stress put on families by demanding older parents and grandparents in the churches I served. I chose to try to be reasonable. While the desire to stay in familiar surroundings was screaming in my ears on one hand, the willingness to respond to wisdom and good judgement won out on the other. The decision was made to move closer to family. More losses and more grief followed, all because a thief had slowly taken Jan from us. I continued to pray as tears dampened my pillow at night.

Looking back, I know this was the hardest decision I made during Jan's Alzheimer's. With each change came more losses. This move cost me the longstanding friendships of a church fellowship. It meant leaving a lovely home and many caring neighbors. I was starting over in unfamiliar surroundings. Jan and I had moved many times in our sixty-six years of marriage, but we had done it together. Jan's gift of hospitality and her love of people helped us adjust to each new town and home. This time I had to do it alone, as an eighty-eight-year-old man. It was devastating. These words of Jesus came to mind:

Come to me, all you who are weary and burdened,
and I will give you rest. Take my yoke upon you
and learn from me, for I am gentle and humble
in heart, and you will find rest for your souls. For
my yoke is easy and my burden is light.

Matthew 11:28-30

Gradually, I placed my burdens upon Jesus, and He began to give me rest. I don't mean to imply that everything was easy after that. It was hard, but I knew that Father God would see me through.

A few days before moving day, our bedroom was quiet except for Jan's deep breathing. It was 3:00 a.m. I was sitting in my comfortable chair after taking Jan to the bathroom. Peace began to edge out the feelings of disappointment about the coming move. The hymn by Annie Johnson Flint, "What God Hath Promised," started to play in my inner mind. I silently hummed the tune and mouthed the words like Jan and I had done so many times. I could almost see Annie Flint with her arthritic twisted body and gnarled hands, lying on her bed, with chalk wedged between her fingers, writing these words on paper attached to a board suspended above her. I decided my situation was not so bad after all. These words spoke volumes to me that morning:

God has not promised skies always blue,
Flower-strewn pathways all our lives through;
God has not promised sun without rain,
Joy without sorrow, peace without pain.

But God has promised strength for the day,
Rest for the labor, light for the way,
Grace for the trials, help from above,
Unfailing kindness, undying love.

Janette found a highly recommended memory care facility near her home for Jan, and we established a care package to meet her needs. I would have an adequate independent living apartment in an adjacent building. A move date was set and a moving company scheduled. I decided to look forward to what was ahead rather than brooding over my losses. I was successful most of the time, but I do admit I struggled. It seemed like I was letting Jan down.

We were up early on moving day. Excellent planning for the move had been done by our family. It was time to go. With sadness in my heart, we got Jan in the front seat next to Janette who would be our driver. I settled into the back seat. We drove through a torrential rainstorm causing my anxiety to heighten. As we drew near our destination, I took a deep breath and thought, *Now we will be all right. Jan will be cared for by trained professionals.* I wondered what they would think of what I had been doing with no training or skills.

We arrived at Clear Sky Haven mid-day of August 24, 2018. Distance had made it impossible for me to visit this facility earlier, so everything was new to me. Clear Sky was an attractive well-kept facility. It included an extensive area for independent living, a section for assisted living, a large long-term care center and a memory care unit. Jan's new home would be an efficiency apartment in memory care. Upon arrival, we were ushered into an attractive conference room. We were tired from the trip and we knew the moving van would be arriving soon. The nurse guided us through Jan's admission process. It seemed like we were rehashing the same paperwork I had completed, signed, and emailed to the facility the week before. Janette took Jan to a lounge area where she was able to care for her needs and have a snack.

Next, I met with the housing counselor to complete more paperwork. I was exhausted and frustrated as we went over document after document that I had prepared and sent in advance. The person helping me didn't seem to know I had pre-arranged everything. I tried to explain, but she continued on as if no pre-registration had occurred. This experience was reminiscent of the earlier event when registering at assisted living. Administrators, I urge you to consider how you can receive new residents in a way that will ease the difficult transition for them.

It had been a tough day. I stood in the living room of my new home, tired and bewildered. Boxes were stacked in every vacant corner. Janette and John helped me get settled enough to get through the night. I didn't feel much like eating. They left and loneliness consumed me. Prayer was far away. I flipped to chapter 1 of the Gospel of John on my phone, but my mind wouldn't receive it. Sleep came, and morning was a new day. I tried to think of moving day as a positive step, but it seemed like a "bad day." I remembered the time Jan had reminded me,

"Don't call it a bad day. God made it." I smiled and tears of love rolled down my face. My resolve returned. With the help of the memory care staff, I determined to continue to care for Jan as long as she lived.

Father God,
please enfold in your love people
who are living in care centers.
May they be treated
with dignity and respect.
Empower those who care for them
with your mercy and grace.
Amen

CHAPTER 12

A Long Cold Winter

The next day, a Saturday, I decide to wait until early afternoon to visit Jan. When I arrived at her apartment, I found her on the floor calling, "Help me, help me!" I don't know how long she had been lying there. I clicked her call button to get help and tried to comfort her while we waited. About ten minutes later an aide arrived. Seeing Jan on the floor, she panicked. She knew there was a clipboard in the unit that detailed specific steps that must be followed before she was allowed to get Jan up from the hard floor. Several minutes passed as she scrambled to locate the clipboard. A few more minutes were spent looking for her pen. Finally, she started on the checklist.

Fortunately, an off-duty aide happened by and, seeing the situation, sat down on the floor, held Jan's head and shoulders on her lap, and comforted her. She saw my bewilderment and reassured me. Questioning if we had chosen the right place for Jan's care, I thought, *How can this be happening on the very first day?*

After taking Jan's vitals, making several phone calls, and

checking for pain, the aide was given permission to get her up. A mechanical lift arrived. Clearly frightened by the device, Jan looked to me for help. In frustration, I left the room, partly because I couldn't bear seeing my beautiful wife dangling in the air, fear written all over her face, and partly to get out of the way of the aides. From the hallway, I could hear the aides talking loudly about something completely unrelated to Jan's care. I thought, *Some soft, kind words of comfort and reassurance would be helpful right now.* When the aides were finished, I returned to the room to find Jan sitting in her recliner with her shawl around her shoulders. She welcomed me with a smile as if nothing had happened.

This was my introduction to memory care. Obviously, the aide on duty was not equipped to meet the needs of residents in memory care. I kept thinking, *God, what have I done bringing Jan here?* Finding, training, and retaining qualified nurses' aides, at the salaries a facility is willing to pay, is a major problem. Throughout our stay in memory care, there were several instances of staffing shortages, allowing time for only the minimum care of bathroom needs, food service, and repositioning. I remember one weekend evening when the only staff on duty was one sixteen-year-old aide at a time of day when residents were in the dining room, needing assistance getting back to their apartments. This is an unsafe situation and should not be allowed to happen.

I mention these things out of concern, not criticism. The facility management was doing everything possible to address the problems. With the coming increase in memory care patients, these issues must be resolved. Funds are needed to bring about a better staff to resident ratio and for better training of personnel.

During the first month in memory care, Jan fell three more times, usually as a result of trying to get out of her recliner by herself. At a nurse's suggestion, I purchased a different style of recliner, but she fell out of it as well. I know that Jan was trying to get up because she was not content to be alone for long periods of time. I was also frustrated by not knowing my role. I didn't know if I was free to help with Jan's care. I wondered if I would be seen as interfering with the responsibilities of the care staff. When I raised these questions in the pre-admission process, I was told, "Don't worry about it, we'll take good care of her."

I would have welcomed some specific guidelines regarding my role while Jan was in memory care. I assumed memory care meant the resident would be cared for twenty-four hours a day. I thought I would be a visitor when I arrived at Jan's apartment. After Jan was admitted and had fallen a couple of times, an aide looked at me with some frustration and said, "This is assisted living memory care. We can't watch over your wife every minute of the day." I had expected that my role as Jan's caregiver would be passed to the agency we had chosen to care for her. Why wouldn't I think that from the wording of her care package and the bill I would be paying each month? I was looking forward to coming and going with confidence that Jan was safe and comfortable when I was away.

Noticing my frustration, one of the more experienced aides took our daughter and me aside and explained the difference between *assisted living memory care* and *long term memory care*. She took us to the long term memory care unit so we could see how it functioned. She helped us understand that our participation in Jan's care while in assisted living memory care was not only allowed, but appreciated. That was a very helpful answer to the question I had been asking since before our arrival.

We decided Jan was in the better of the two memory care options. Once I understood my role, we found a workable routine, and I was pleased to be involved in Jan's care, making it possible for me to continue to keep the personal vow I had made to care for Jan as long as she lived. I was willing and happy to spend quality time with her each day. To compensate for staff shortages on weekends, I spent more time with Jan on Saturdays and Sundays. Often, I would leave a note asking the staff to have Jan ready for chapel when I arrived on Sunday afternoon. At this point in her decline, Jan was still able to sing along with the hymns and enjoy being with people.

As long as I was able to transfer Jan to the wheelchair, she enjoyed going outside for a ride in the garden. However, in less than a month, it was determined that it was unsafe to transfer Jan without the use of a mechanical lift. This required two aides for safety purposes. Most of the time there were only two aides on duty to care for about twenty residents. That meant both aides were needed to transfer Jan from one position to another.

Needless to say, we did a lot of waiting and often the need was well past urgent before help arrived.

Gradually, after several care conferences with administrative and nursing staff, we worked out a plan of shared care, and Jan adjusted to her new home. Since most of the group activities were held in the morning, I decided to spend afternoons with Jan. On most days, she would sleep part of the time. We played music and read the Bible and other books. I was there to see that her personal needs were met and that she received her medication before dinner time. Sometimes I would leave for an hour or so while Jan was in the dining room for dinner. One evening, I returned after dinner to find Jan sitting in her wheelchair in the doorway of another apartment anxiously trying to push herself either in or out. I went to help her. The aide said Jan was anxious and another resident needed help, so she had to bring Jan with her. This illustrates the inadequacy of two aides for twenty residents during the busy time of day. Multiply this by the predicted increase in the number of older people with Alzheimer's in the coming years and the result is a major problem. The increase in the cost of adequate staffing for memory care will deplete the resources of many families, putting the burden on state and county budgets.

People with Alzheimer's are so vulnerable that it is easy to neglect them thinking they aren't aware of what is happening to them. That is all the more reason to ensure that their care provides for their comfort and dignity. On numerous occasions, things like Jan's medication schedule or changes in diet would have gone unnoticed if I had not been there to remind the aides of her needs. I wonder what gets neglected for patients who have no one to advocate for them. It has been over a century since Alzheimer's was given a name and still no effective treatments have been found. Rather than continuing to spend so much money on research, let's put our effort into caring for people with Alzheimer's in a way that preserves their self-respect.

Autumn of 2018 was slipping into winter. We considered hiring a van to transport Jan to our daughter's home for our family's Thanksgiving gathering. After much discussion, we decided to have her stay at her apartment, and family members took turns visiting her throughout the afternoon. The first Thanksgiving without Grandma was another loss and the cause of some tears. Yet, we were able to express our thanks for a woman of quality and honor.

Minnesota winters can be challenging. My apartment was a mile and a half from the building where Jan lived. No garage meant brushing snow from my car, sometimes twice a day. We were "blessed" with an unusual amount of snow that winter. Temperatures dipped as low as -40 degrees Fahrenheit. The only day my car failed to start was the day my grandson was visiting. He took care of the problem with little delay, and we went to spend some time with Jan. I felt God's care through the winter.

In January 2019, the medical staff started to indicate it was time to consider admitting Jan to hospice care. I held off for a while, remembering that she had been on hospice earlier and had to be removed when there weren't enough visible signs of decline. Toward the end of January we chose a hospice agency, and Jan was admitted to their care. I cannot speak highly enough about the quality of our hospice experience. The health aide was skilled, kind, and understanding. Jan responded to her assistance with her beautiful smiles. The nurses were compassionate and willing to listen to my concerns and answer my questions. The music therapist lifted our spirits.

On Valentine's Day, 2019, my daughter and I had a conference with the hospice nurse. She shared her observations and explained the decisions they were making for Jan's comfort. When she asked if we had concerns, I was ready with a list I had written the night before. After starting with some routine questions, I asked the *big one*.

"I know you can't answer this question," I said, "but, in your experience, where do you think we are in the progression of Jan's Alzheimer's? Do you see signs of decline? Do you expect Jan will continue as she is now for a long period of time? It's getting increasingly hard to see her just sit and sleep or pretend to sleep because she can't do anything else. I know there are no certain answers, but I would like to know what you think we may expect over the next months."

Without hesitation, the hospice nurse responded, "Sure, let's talk about that. You are right, we have no conclusive answers, but I am certainly willing to share with you my observations over the few weeks we have been with you. If you are wondering how long Jan may live in her present condition, I would say she has months, not years. I doubt that it will be a matter of weeks. She likely will see the spring flowers, but probably not the color of fall leaves. That is the best I can do because only God knows for sure."

Tears spilled down my face as I looked at her and said, "Thank you for being direct with me. Knowing what you have said, gives me new resolve to keep on through this long cold winter knowing that spring will come. This dreadful thief has robbed her of her memory, but it will not have her soul. I know she will have the victory in the end. Winter is cold and dark, but spring will be bright and clear."

I reached my hand to the nurse and thanked her for her honesty and said, "I won't hold you to what you have said, but it lifts a burden from my shoulders. This has been a long journey over the last ten years. At least we can begin to see our destination."

That winter evening, after driving home to the loneliness of my apartment, I started a music DVD to fill the quietness. The song by John M. Moore, "Burdens Are Lifted at Calvary" came on. An avalanche of tears stored up over the ten years of watching Thief *Alzheimer's* diminish my lovely wife to total helplessness, broke loose as I realized I could trust that burden to the death of Jesus at Calvary. Listen to the words:

> Days are filled with sorrow and care,
> Hearts are lonely and drear.
> Burdens are lifted at Calvary,
> Jesus is very near.
>
> Burdens are lifted at Calvary, Calvary, Calvary;
> Burdens are lifted at Calvary, Jesus is very near.

Through the tears, I was reminded that Calvary could not hold Jesus. On the third day he broke free from the grave. I could begin to see the end of a long journey. Some day in the not too distant future, Jan would be set free from the bondage of nothingness. Yes, burdens are lifted at Calvary. I was ready for what seemed like the last lap of a long race. Then suddenly, like a flash of light, I thought of all the people who have tread this same journey. For some, it has been longer and harder. I thought of all who will find themselves on this uncertain road in the future, millions of travelers dealing with the same issues. I could only pray that they will travel with Jesus while drinking from the endless supply of living water.

Hospice provided a Broda wheelchair for Jan, allowing her to sit or recline in a variety of more comfortable positions. The hospice dietitian helped Jan with some meals and made recommendations for softer foods and thickened drinks, making it easier for her to swallow. Jan responded to the music therapist and often sang along. Burdens were lifted from my shoulders as hospice became a wonderful gift.

I adjusted my visits as we worked with hospice. The hospice aides were scheduled in the morning, so I continued to arrive in early afternoon and stayed until Jan was settled for the night. Much of the time I sat next to her wheelchair, held her hand and told her how much I loved her, but she rarely responded. Her eyes grew distant or were closed most of the time.

Great Grandson, Trey, "What's the matter, Great Grandma?"

Late in the afternoon, Jan often became restless and fidgety in her wheelchair. She would look at her bed, but didn't have words to express her wishes. A mild anti-anxiety medication helped her settle down enough to eat the evening meal. Jan's decline was such that she no longer had control of her hands and arms. I brought her dinner tray to her room and fed her the evening meal. I had to touch the spoon to her lips to remind her to open her mouth for each bite. I doubt she had any sense of taste. Often, she refused to open her mouth, turning her head to the side. I kept a few of her favorite foods in the refrigerator and sometimes I could get her to take a few more bites by mixing in some canned fruit. Mealtime required patience and endurance.

After supper, I would take Jan for a ride in her wheelchair, strolling up and down the halls. She didn't know where she was, but she seemed to like the movement and change of scene. In the cold of winter we enjoyed a stop by the fireplace in the lounge to listen to music. The ride would end at the chapel where I read with her and we would hum some hymns together. One of the last things she was able to do was to pray the Lord's Prayer with me. Every evening, for months, I read the first four verses of Hebrews chapter one with her:

> In the past God spoke to our ancestors through the prophets at many times and in various ways, but in these last days he has spoken to us by his Son, whom he appointed heir of all things, and through whom also he made the universe. The Son is the radiance of God's glory and the exact representation of his being, sustaining all things by his powerful word. After he had provided purification for sins, he sat down at the right hand of the Majesty in heaven. So he became as much superior to the angels as the name he has inherited is superior to theirs.
>
> Hebrews 1:1-4

I talked to Jan about our wonderful Savior. Sometimes she nodded in agreement. I told her about heaven and that Jesus is there at the right hand of God praying for us. Sometimes she would smile when I talked about the place Jesus had prepared in heaven for us. We prayed that Jesus would allow her to come to His heaven before me so I could help care for her until she went to be with Jesus. This was such a wonderful time each day. Sometimes she would see the tears on my face and look at me with puzzlement, not understanding why I was crying.

Sometimes we would laugh as I told of a special memory. These were short times, but so very special.

With a little lighter heart, we arrived back at her apartment, her head hung with drowsiness longing to get into her bed. I flossed and brushed her teeth, washed and put lotion on her face. I counted it a privilege to do these things to make her a little more comfortable. While waiting for the aides to finish the process of getting Jan into bed, I rubbed her feet with lotion, humming a favorite hymn. We ended the day with a Bible verse and prayer much like a parent would with a child. I made sure not to treat her like a child. Remembering her deep faith and trust in Jesus helped me treat her like the beautiful, graceful woman I had married sixty-seven years before.

Gradually the snowdrifts of the long cold winter gave way to the brighter days of springtime. I noticed the ice breaking up on the river as I crossed the bridge on my way to visit my beloved. A wheelchair ride in the garden gave Jan a chance to see the flowers announce the arrival of spring. The words of the hospice nurse came to mind, "She likely will see the spring flowers, but probably not the color of fall leaves." For Jan's sake, I prayed that the days would be shortened before her arrival at the place Jesus had prepared for her.

As spring warmed toward summer, Jan's twin sister, Joanne, fell and was admitted to the hospital. She died on May 28, 2019. By this time, Jan was eating very little. Swallowing was difficult, and her body wasn't digesting her food. Her brain was shutting down. A few days later, I called our sons and daughters together. We were nearing the end of our long journey from the first indications of memory loss to Jan's arrival at her heavenly home. As I prepared to say goodbye to Jan, the words of the Apostle Paul took on fresh meaning:

> I have fought the good fight, I have finished the race, I have kept the faith. Now there is in store for me the crown of righteousness, which the Lord, the righteous Judge, will award to me on that day—and not only to me, but also to all who have longed for his appearing.
>
> 2 Timothy 4:7-8

Blessed
are those who mourn,
for
they will be comforted,

———⊰⊱———

MATTHEW 5:4

CHAPTER 13

A New Road Beginning

It was morning, June 5, 2019. The room was still except for her deep breathing. Multitudes of memories were flying through my mind. It had been a long journey, and the time had come for her to say, "I have fought the good fight, I have finished the race, I have kept the faith." Her acts of kindness, her words of encouragement, her steady support in times of despair, her gentle touch, and her soft winning smile were all finished. Family had gathered. The hospice nurse had said, "When her breathing rate goes below twenty it won't be long." I counted, one, two, three, and on to twenty-three. I stepped away from her bed, and Paul sat down by his mom. A few minutes later, from across the room, Paul said, "Dad, it's at thirteen." I knelt by her bed. Family around me. Her breathing stilled. She was at peace. I touched her face. Thoughts came of times we talked and prayed together. I quoted the words we had spoken so many times over the fading years of her Alzheimer's, "O God our help in ages past, our hope for years to come. Our shelter from the stormy blast, and our eternal home." Her work on earth was done, and she was ready for her heavenly reward. I closed her eyes.

It had been a long, hard road. We had often reassured each other with the comfort of knowing where the road would lead. Shortly after Jan died, a poem began to form in my mind. I had never thought of writing poetry, so it is simple and lacks polish, but it speaks my thoughts.

A NEW ROAD BEGINNING
By Marvin Eppard, in honor of his wife Janice

A road stretched out ahead of us,
Not knowing what a day would bring.
We did what we did yesterday,
The music played and I heard her sing.

She tried so hard to express herself,
With words no longer remembered.
But a hymn that came from deep within,
Could say what her heart still treasured.

Time slipped past as memory failed,
The hymns brought only a smile.
She was left with but the tap of toe,
Eyes closed, as she listened a while.

Thirty minutes the therapist played,
She lay there as if sound asleep.
A touch, her name her husband spoke,
Eyes opened; no more did slumber keep.

"How great Thou art," the therapist began,
Forgotten voice returned.
Together they sang the resounding words,
Sweeter than ever was heard.

The smile on her face the therapist saw,
Like sunshine in a dreary place.
"You are my sunshine," the therapist sang,
She followed with excited pace.

The therapist quietly left the room.
She lay there deep in thought.
We waited in a room so still,
A holy presence, God wrought.

She spoke, after months of silence,
These words of jubilation.
With strong voice she declared,
"That was a celebration."

"It sure was," her husband agreed,
Speaking with all sincerity.
He waited, she lingered,
It seemed like an eternity.

She asked the question with excitement,
Pondered thought with brow furrowed.
"Do you know Jesus?" she inquired,
As if asking it of all the world.

"I sure do," her husband answered,
"And so do you," he said with assurance.
She smiled with beauty from deep within,
Waiting in thought of some endurance.

With deep breath she drew in certainty,
"That makes my heart jump," she said firmly.
Suddenly she returned to earlier slumber,
Having spoken words the world needs terribly.

The road seemed to end a few days later,
He closed her eyes with fingers trembling.
Vows had been kept he knew from within,
Our Father beckoned; a new road is beginning.

Then reality set in. After sixty-seven years of marriage and nearly ten years of caring for Jan as she slowly drifted farther and farther away, I was suddenly alone. I struggled to find a balance between the grief of loss and the peace of knowing that Jan was free. A new road was beginning for me.

The new road for Jan is in heaven, where Jesus had prepared a place for her. She had no doubt about where she would be when she died, and she wanted to help other people have the same assurance. In my last conversation with her,

Jan asked me, "Do you know Jesus?" She asked that question of many people in her eighty-seven years—particularly of children. It makes me smile to think about how many people will be in heaven because of her kind words and loving teaching. Even in the deepest decline of her Alzheimer's, she would smile when I talked with her about heaven. Jan's beauty showed through in the simplicity of her trust in Jesus and His promises.

The road Jan travels now gives me peace and courage to travel on my new road. I miss her every day, but I would not wish her back. She is free from the darkness of her Alzheimer's. I'm reminded of the stanza in the song, "Knowing What I Know About Heaven," by Guy Penrod,

> I could hope that I could pray you're back
> But why on earth would I do that
> When you're somewhere, life and love never ends
> Oh, knowing what I know about heaven

We know a lot about heaven. The word "heaven" appears in the Bible over six hundred times. The Bible is the place to go to find the truth. When Jesus was on trial before Pilate, He said, "in fact, the reason I was born and came into the world is to testify to the truth. Everyone on the side of truth listens to me" (John 18:37b). Shortly before He was crucified, Jesus spoke these words of comfort and truth to His disciples:

Do not let your hearts be troubled. You believe in God; believe also in me. My Father's house has many rooms; if that were not so, would I have told you that I am going there to prepare a *place* for you? And if I go and prepare a *place* for you, I will come back and take you to be with me that you also may be where I am. You know the way to the *place* where I am going.

John 14:1-4

Heaven is a place, a real place, not some spiritual, ethereal concept. It is Father God's place of residence. Heaven is where God is. Jesus said, "This, then, is how you should pray: 'Our *Father in heaven*, hallowed be your name . . .'" (Matthew 6:9). When we pray, we are addressing Father God in heaven. When Jesus was teaching His followers to let their light shine and not hide it under a bowl, He said, "In the same way, let your light shine before others, that they may see your good deeds and glorify your *Father in heaven*" (Matthew 5:16).

Jesus was a master teacher. By making the assumption that his disciples would know the way to the place He had prepared for them in heaven, he guided them to ask the important questions. Thomas voiced what they were all probably thinking when he asked, "Lord, we don't know where you are going, so how can we know the way?" (John 14:5).

Jesus gave a simple, but profound answer, "I am the way and the truth and the life. No one comes to the Father except through me. If you really know me, you know my Father as well. From now on, you do know him and have seen him" (John 14:6-7). Knowing Jesus is the way to know the Father, for they are one. Jesus, by the Holy Spirit, inspired four of his followers, Matthew, Mark, Luke, and John, to write clear accounts of the life of Jesus so we can know the way to the Father's house. Reading them over and over will help you know Jesus, who is The Way.

Our Father in heaven desires that all of His creation would be with Him in His heavenly home. He doesn't want any to be lost. To provide a way for all the world to be with Him, God sent His Son, Immanuel, to live among us. Heaven's angels announced His birth in Bethlehem. He became a human being like us. Jesus left his home with Father God in heaven so that we could know Him, the One who is the way to heaven.

A few years ago, I happened to find a church website where the preacher referred to this passage as "the most terrible, horrible passage in all Scripture," because, in the preacher's opinion, it is exclusive. The preacher contended that if Jesus is the only way to heaven, many people would be excluded. The preacher used passages from contemporary authors as evidence of the exclusiveness of these words of Jesus.

I would say the exact opposite. The God of all creation loved the world so much that he sent His Son from heaven to suffer a horrible, sacrificial death on a cross to pay the penalty for the sins of all mankind. His Son died, and three days later, rose from the grave. For forty days after his resurrection, He appeared in a real body, truly alive, so everyone can know He is the victory over death. Jesus reached across the chasm between mankind and God and gave us all the way to eternal life with the Father. What could be more inclusive than that?

I wonder what heaven is like for Jan. It must be an adventure. The Bible gives some insight into what heaven is like, but there's little doubt that images of streets of gold, jewel laden foundations, gates of pearl, and angelic choirs fall short of what heaven is like. The Apostle Paul tells of being caught up to the third heaven,

> I know a man in Christ who fourteen years ago was caught up to the third heaven. Whether it was in the body or out of the body I do not know—God knows. And I know that this man—whether in the body or apart from the body I do not know, but God knows—was caught up to paradise and heard inexpressible things, things that no one is permitted to tell.
>
> 2 Corinthians 12:2-4

Paul was so overwhelmed by this experience that apparently he had not shared it until fourteen years later and still did not describe it as his own. It is obvious that he is writing about himself. Whatever Paul saw and experienced in his glimpse into heaven, it was so vivid that it was inexpressible. Paul, a master of words, was speechless. Jan is there now, and I am thrilled to know that she is filled with joy. I look forward to the day when I will join her. Paul may have been remembering his vision when he wrote,

For to me, to live is Christ and to die is gain. If
I am to go on living in the body, this will mean
fruitful labor for me. Yet what shall I choose? I
do not know! I am torn between the two: I desire
to depart and be with Christ, which is better by
far; but it is more necessary for you that I remain
in the body.

Philippians 1:21-24

These words encouraged me when the days got long as
I cared for Jan. Often I prayed that she would be set free to
be with Jesus. That would be gain for her. Yet, until that day
came, I trusted God to give me the strength and resolve to go
on caring for her.

David Jeremiah tells a wonderful story about a Sunday
School teacher who is teaching her class about heaven. The
teacher asks her class, "If I sell everything I have and give to
the poor, will that get me into heaven?" The children all shout,
"No! No!" The teacher goes on and asks, "If I take good care of
my house and tend my gardens and lawn perfectly, will that get
me into heaven?" Again, the resounding "No! No!" The teacher,
remembering how much the children love their pets, asked, "If
I am kind to animals and treat my family and neighbors with
respect and kindness, will that get me into heaven?" Again, the
shouts of "No! No!" "How then will I get to go to heaven?" she
asked. The class became silent. Then a boy toward the back of
the room who was new to the class, responded firmly, "You
have to be dead."

That's true, and at some point, all of us will meet that first requirement. The question is, where will we be after we die? The Bible is clear that everyone will have eternal life, either in heaven with Jesus, or separated from Him in hell. Jesus said, "But I will show you whom you should fear: Fear him who, after your body has been killed, has authority to throw you into hell. Yes, I tell you, fear him" (Luke 12:5). In Revelation, the One seated on the throne in heaven says,

> It is done. I am the Alpha and the Omega, the Beginning and the End. To the thirsty I will give water without cost from the spring of the water of life. Those who are victorious will inherit all this, and I will be their God and they will be my children. But the cowardly, the unbelieving, the vile, the murderers, the sexually immoral, those who practice magic arts, the idolaters and all liars—they will be consigned to the fiery lake of burning sulfur. This is the second death.
>
> Revelation 21:6-8

We don't like to think about a place called hell, but the Bible clearly teaches that Satan desires to claim people for his kingdom, and that kingdom is hell.

Jesus has made a place for everyone in heaven. The question is, have you made a reservation for the place He has for you? Jesus has done His part. He came from heaven and assured us that the price has been paid. Our part is to accept His gift.

Imagine with me that the most marvelous, most spectacular

concert is scheduled to be held in your city. Your all-time favorite music will be performed by world-renowned artists who are so popular that you would never be able to pay the price of a ticket. You only can dream about what it would be like to attend. Then you get a letter telling you that someone has purchased a front-row ticket for you, and you can go for free. You are so surprised that you think it's a hoax. You resist every effort of your friends to assure you it's real. The letter explains that your benefactor wants you to change some of your priorities and spend time getting to know him personally before the concert. The letter says that accepting the gift will change your life and give you contentment and joy.

You think about it briefly and decide not to accept. You like your life the way it is, and you don't want to change anything. When the day of the concert comes, you find out that the One who offered the ticket to you has done the same thing for everyone else. There were enough front-row tickets for everyone. Suddenly you find yourself at the gate. You can hear the music begin to play inside. Up ahead you can see an attendant looking for each person's name in a book. The people with reservations in the book, are ushered in to the concert. Anyone whose name is not found in the book is sent to a place of darkness so dark it is like coals of fire. Is this real? The Bible says it is very real:

> Then I saw a great white throne and him who
> was seated on it. The earth and the heavens
> fled from his presence, and there was no place

for them. And I saw the dead, great and small, standing before the throne, and books were opened. Another book was opened, which is the book of life. The dead were judged according to what they had done as recorded in the books. The sea gave up the dead that were in it, and death and Hades gave up the dead that were in them, and each person was judged according to what they had done. Then death and Hades were thrown into the lake of fire. The lake of fire is the second death. Anyone whose name was not found written in the book of life was thrown into the lake of fire.

Revelation 20:11-15

Is your name in the book? It can be. The price of your reservation has already been paid! If you want to know that your name is in God's book in heaven, you can start by praying a prayer something like this:

Lord Jesus, I know I need You. I want to be with You for all eternity. I have known about You, but now I want to know You. I ask you to forgive my sin. I surrender my life to you and ask you to renew my mind. Give me assurance that You have a place for me in heaven. Amen

Jan made that decision when she was nine years old. She received the gift early in her life and that relationship continued to grow all through her life. As she matured as a Christ-follower, she became more able to help others find Jesus. "Do you know Jesus?" she would ask with a smile.

We all have an eternity ahead of us. What could be better than living it with Jesus? Heaven is to be where Jesus is in God's house. In heaven, we will see his nail pierced hands reminding us of what He has done as the way and the truth and the life. I know Jan is there. If she could, she would ask you, "Do you know Jesus?"

*"And we know
that in all things God works
for the good
of those who love him,
who have been called according
to his purpose"*

—⊷⧢⊶—

ROMANS 8:28

CHAPTER 14

God Working For Good

A year-and-a-half have passed since Jan died. I often think of the much quoted verse, "And we know that in all things God works for the good of those who love him, who have been called according to his purpose" (Romans 8:28). That verse says ". . . in *all* things," not *some* things, so that means God was at work in my life throughout that challenging ten-year span. One thing is certain, He awakened in me the realization that sixty-seven years of marriage with Jan was a wonderful gift. Would I want some things to have been different? Of course I would. I certainly wish that Jan didn't have to experience the slow decline of Alzheimer's. I wish I could have cared for her at home all the way to her death. I wish a lot of things could have been different, but those wishes aren't helpful. Instead, I would rather focus on the valuable lessons that I discovered through this experience. In this chapter, I count it a privilege to share the good things that God accomplished in my life while caring for Jan.

One gigantic gain for me is to know that Jan is in the place of her true citizenship. The Bible teaches that this earth is our temporary home. "But our citizenship is in heaven. And we eagerly await a Savior from there, the Lord Jesus Christ" (Philippians 3:20). Through the experience of caring for Jan, I was able to allow God to loosen my grip on this life and release Jan to His care. I am thankful.

The monotony of the days made it difficult to recognize at the time, but during the ten years of caring for Jan, I made wonderful discoveries about marriage. Knowing what I know now, I am not surprised that so many marriages end in divorce. Early in our marriage, I was extremely selfish. I did not intend to be selfish. I was selfish because of the needs I brought to our marriage. It is hard, if not impossible, to enter marriage as an unselfish person when we are self-centered by nature. If Jan and I had not been willing to allow God to work in our hearts to be *givers* rather than *takers,* I never would have been able to care for her over the long haul. Looking back, I can see the miraculous work of God to overcome our selfishness and make us one.

To be able to love Jan unselfishly in her need was a marvelous discovery. When I was helping her with all her basic needs, I came to realize I was doing it because I valued her as a gift from God. I often thought of the words of 1 John 4:19, "We love because he first loved us." Many times, when the going was hard, God reminded me that His Son, Jesus, loved me enough to give His life upon the cross to pay the price of my sin that I might have life with Him forever. I began to view caring for

Jan as a gift from God. This alone made the ten years more valuable than gold.

Difficult days strengthened the bond God had brought about in our lives together, and in the process, I grew to admire Jan beyond words. Helping her with all of the things she could not do for herself, caused me to realize what "being made one" truly meant. Seeing her give as much as she could, even if it was only a whispered "Thank you," I saw in vivid fashion what oneness means. Being empowered to do things that seemed impossible, revealed the joy of being one with my wife. I gained new understanding of the words Jesus quoted,

> 'Haven't you read,' he replied, 'that at the beginning the Creator made them male and female,' and said, 'For this reason a man will leave his father and mother and be united to his wife, and the two will become one flesh'? So they are no longer two, but one flesh. Therefore what God has joined together, let no one separate.'
>
> Matthew 19:4-6

As Jan lost more and more of the ability to do things for herself, it became necessary for me to do more and more for her, and the days grew more demanding for me. But, because God had made us one, I was able to shoulder that burden willingly. I discovered that when I surrendered my life to God, He would give me strength to carry the load for both of us. I'm not saying this was easy. Many times, the burden became nearly unbearable. In the later years, I appealed to God often to take Jan Home. Yet, He sustained us to go on, one day at a time.

Also, during this ten-year journey, God taught me many things about love. It is easy to love when you get as much in return. Many people believe marriage is a 50/50 deal. Jesus said, "If you love those who love you, what reward will you get? Are not even the tax collectors doing that?" (Matthew 5:46). Real love is not about what we get in return. Real love is loving when we get nothing in return. I fell in love with Jan before we started dating. If ever there was "love at first sight," it happened to me. But that was not mature love. As friends, before we started dating, I grew to respect and admire Jan. Over the years, our love for each other grew stronger as we supported and honored each other. When the time came that Jan needed constant care, I was able to draw on the depth of our relationship to do the things she could not do for herself. As we moved along I began to realize how much I loved her. Love became mature because it required nothing in return. My love for her desired everything for her out of everything that God gave to me. This is why it hurt me so much when I watched her lose her dignity in the later stages of Alzheimer's.

During this long journey, I discovered a lot about myself. As Jan's abilities decreased, I had to increase. As she lost the ability to do the things she had always done, I had to pick up the slack. I began to realize how much I had been taking her for granted. As I first realized this, I felt ashamed for the way I had treated the one I loved. Then I began to think of the things I had done for both of us and could have resented being taken for granted.

As I understood how much we relied upon each other, great joy came into my heart. That's what marriage should be. Jan was a wonderful homemaker. I had gifts for managing our finances. She wrote hundreds of cards and letters. I took care of the yard and shoveled the snow. The more I realized the oneness that we had, the more I grew in my love for her. This made caring for her far more an act of love than a burden to bear.

The loss of my mother when I was three-years-old left a gaping hole in my life. I know now that I spent several years of our marriage trying to find ways to fill that emptiness. I tried to draw from Jan the love I had missed from my mother. She could not love me like a mother, but, thankfully, she was emotionally and spiritually strong enough to help me through those years. I believe that I met some of the needs in her life because God was in the process of making us one. Fortunately, Jan and I had great respect for one another from the beginning, and we allowed God to work that oneness in our marriage. Many marriages fail because the partners are unwilling to give up self to become one with each other.

My severe reading disability caused insecurity and lack of confidence in most areas of my life. In high school, excelling in sports helped me gain confidence, but that came to an abrupt end when I graduated. Later, I took up wood working and found confidence in my ability to build things from canoes to custom cabinetry. Jan understood my lack of confidence and her encouragement helped me to draw my confidence from God's plan for my life.

I also made discoveries about forgiveness. Sometimes, when the burden of Jan's constant needs and demands would cause me to reach the end of my rope, I would explode with frustration. I was careful not to lash out *at* her; however there were times when I stomped off in an adult tantrum. Then guilt would begin to condemn me. My old insecurities would burst in upon me. To keep from putting the blame on Jan, I would become critical of other people. It didn't matter who; I would just find anyone I could blame. We didn't have a dog, or I would have blamed the dog. Eventually, I learned to take these times to Jesus, remembering when He said, "For if you forgive other people when they sin against you, your heavenly Father will also forgive you. But if you do not forgive others their sins, your Father will not forgive your sins" (Matthew 6:14-15). I would ask Jan to forgive me. She would smile and nod her head. Knowing that was all she could do, I would put my arms around her and say, "Thank you, my dear lady."

Another lesson that Jan taught me during this journey was the value of thanksgiving. Every little thing I did for her brought the words, "Thank you." These two magical words were among the last to leave her. It is amazing what those two words can do to ease a heavy load. Jan's continual thankfulness, has caused me to express thanks to others far more than before. It has changed my prayer life as I have become more and more aware of all Father God means to me. As I receive requests to pray for the needs of others, I often begin by giving thanks for what that person means to me. Praise and thanksgiving always precede the requests.

The bottom drawer of Jan's desk was stocked with Thank You cards. Any act of kindness and every gift we received was acknowledged with an immediate note expressing our appreciation. She lived a life of thanksgiving, following the admonition of the Bible, "Rejoice always, pray continually, give thanks in all circumstances; for this is God's will for you in Christ Jesus" (1 Thessalonians 5:16-18). Since thanksgiving was such a sincere and immediate response throughout her life, it was one of the last to succumb to Alzheimer's.

God was working for good in our lives through it all. As difficult as it was to see Jan's losses, I can see now that the good out-weighed our troubles. Father God was giving me strength for each day and the ability to be thankful for the privilege of being one with Jan as our love for each other matured. Forgiveness released us to meet the demands of each day. I can truly say, "I am thankful." These words from the Apostle Paul sum it up,

> ... being strengthened with all power according to his glorious might so that you may have great endurance and patience, and giving joyful thanks to the Father, who has qualified you to share in the inheritance of his holy people in the kingdom of light. For he has rescued us from the dominion of darkness and brought us into the kingdom of the Son he loves.
>
> Colossians 1:11-13

Forty years ago, if someone had asked, "Marv, would you be willing to clean up nasty messes while caring for your wife?" "No way," would have been my immediate answer. If asked years ago, "Marv, would you be willing to do all the cooking for you and Jan if she were unable to do it?" I would have laughed and answered, "We would never survive." The questions could go on and on. My commitment to care for Jan as long as she lived, had more facets than I ever expected. Yet, I did things I never would have believed I could. How did that happen? There is only one answer and it is not a *trite* answer: *only by the grace of God.* The deep flowing cistern of living water was the abiding source of strength for both Jan and me.

*Thanks
be to God!
He gives us the victory
through
our Lord Jesus Christ.*

———⚬⚬⚬———

1 Corinthians 15:57

CHAPTER 15

Reflections

Writing this love story has caused me to realize how blessed I am. This story doesn't have the exciting, self-gratifying components that would attract the attention of movie producers. Instead, it is a story about what a deep, abiding love can really look like in our needy world. Jan lived her life for other people. I was privileged to be her husband. Jan's oft-asked question, "Do you know Jesus?" was always spoken in love. She knew how much God loved her and she wanted other people to know it too.

This story was written in the midst of the Covid-19 pandemic, rioting in the streets, political in-fighting, and economic uncertainty. Yet none of that can change what we know is true. Jesus truly is God's final Word made known to us in the Bible. He is the Word that became flesh and demonstrated for us the fullness of grace and truth.

I have vivid memories of sitting next to Jan's wheelchair in the chapel in the care center where she spent the last nine months of her life. Thief *Alzheimer's* had so diminished her abilities that she couldn't do much more than smile, but I still read these words with her every evening:

> In the past God spoke to our ancestors through the prophets at many times and in various ways, but in these last days he has spoken to us by his Son, whom he appointed heir of all things, and through whom also he made the universe. The Son is the radiance of God's glory and the exact representation of his being, sustaining all things by his powerful word. After he had provided purification for sins, he sat down at the right hand of the Majesty in heaven. So he became as much superior to the angels as the name he has inherited is superior to theirs.
>
> Hebrews 1:1-4

I wasn't sure how much Jan was comprehending at that point, but I reminded her anyway, "Janie, we are Christ-followers. Jesus was God's final Word to us. God appointed Jesus to inherit everything, so we are followers of the owner of everything. That makes us rich. Jesus is the Word through Whom Father God created everything. That means we are privileged to live in God's wonderful creation. Jesus is the radiance of God's glory. That means we never have to be in darkness. Jesus is exactly like Father God. That means we can know what Father God is like. Jesus holds everything together. That means we don't have to worry about the future. Jesus has made us pure from sin through his death on the cross, so we are forgiven. Now, Jesus is sitting at the right hand of Father God in heaven praying for us. Jesus has a place for us in heaven."

When I spoke about heaven she would smile. She knew heaven was her destination. Like the thief in Grandma's pantry, Alzheimer's will continue to tangle and muddle the memories of millions, but the living water from the cistern offers us assurance of eternal life. As I continue my journey here on earth, I pray that others who are experiencing a similar trial will find comfort and encouragement from knowing Jesus as I do.

To those who are medical caregivers and administrators of care centers, I make a final appeal. Please remember who you are caring for when you encounter victims of Thief *Alzheimer's*. Please preserve their dignity while living in the darkness of dementia. A crisis is in the offing. We need you to apply your skills and influence to help equip your staff on the front lines as they provide the day-to-day care for dementia patients. I am very thankful for the care Jan received, but I know it could be better if we work together to make some needed adjustments.

I have come to the end of my journal. My desk is cleared of all of my notes for this book. Thank you for listening to our story. Thief *Alzheimer's* may think it was the winner in Jan's life, but that is a lie. God is victorious. His Son is the last Word. Jan's life on earth has been completed, but the life she lived will stand as a testimony of true greatness. She fought the good fight, she finished the race, she kept the faith.

Therefore, since we are surrounded by such a great cloud of witnesses, let us throw off everything that hinders and the sin that so easily entangles. And let us run with perseverance the race marked out for us, fixing our eyes on Jesus, the pioneer and perfecter of faith. For the joy set before him he endured the cross, scorning its shame, and sat down at the right hand of the throne of God. Consider him who endured such opposition from sinners, so that you will not grow weary and lose heart.

Hebrews 12:1-3

THE TEA RING LADY

The following tribute to the Tea Ring Lady
was written some months before Jan died.
It is given here as a demonstration of her self-giving life.

4 T yeast

3 ½ cups warm water

½ cup powdered milk

¾ cup sugar

1 T salt

4 eggs

¾ cup butter, melted

½ cup wheat germ

10 cups unbleached flour

½ cup potato flakes

Butter and cinnamon-sugar for filling

Powdered sugar frosting with a touch of lemon

Maraschino cherries

Visitors to the Tea Ring Lady's house were often welcomed with the fragrant aroma of fresh baked bread, sweetened with a touch of cinnamon-sugar and butter. Whatever the occasion—a death in the family of a dear friend; a thank you for an unexpected kindness; a Christmas gift of thanks for our church custodian, office manager, worship and music leaders, or pastor; a special treat for our grandchildren when we visited their home; a tasty addition to a Sunday breakfast when family or friends came to our home for the weekend; a contribution to a church potluck; a delicacy for coffee time at a small group meeting; the list goes on and on. Hundreds of Swedish Tea Rings came out of the Tea Ring Lady's kitchen as sweet offerings of blessing and love to countless people over the years.

I can see her now, standing at the kitchen counter, apron tied around her back, flour on her cheek, and her sleeves rolled up to the elbows. Her glasses have slipped partially down her nose, and determination is in her eyes. The old reliable KitchenAid mixer is plugged in and ready to do its job. The ingredients for the recipe are spread out on the counter, plus one more–the most important ingredient isn't written on the card–it's in the heart of the Tea Ring Lady: a generous helping of love.

Time and again I watched as she mixed and stirred the ingredients together with the big mixing spoon, gradually blending them in the proper order. Soon the KitchenAid started to churn away. I often threatened to buy her a new one, but she liked the old one. Like the Tea Ring Lady herself, it never seemed to quit. Puffs of flour could be seen as she carefully poured cup after cup down the flour chute. Slowly the mixture thickened into a pasty clump. Then came the kneading. I enjoyed the kneading the most. First, she placed the sticky ball of dough on the flour-laden counter; turning it and rolling it into more and more flour. Each turn and punch were followed by a loving pat. More flour, another push, another roll, another pat. Push, roll, punch, and another loving pat.

All the while, off to the side was the old aluminum pan, dented and darkened with use, the inside generously greased with shortening. When the dough was just the right consistency, it was shaped to fit the pan. Then, with a ker-plunk, the rounded ball of dough landed in the pan. The Tea Ring Lady covered it with an old, tattered dish towel to encourage the yeast to perform the miracle of leavening the entire batch of dough.

While the dough is rising, let's think about the ingredients in the Tea Ring Lady's recipe and the ways they reflect characteristics of the lady herself.

Four tablespoons of yeast:

A little yeast brings about change in the whole ball of dough. Again and again, I watched as the genuine love of the Tea Ring Lady changed the attitudes and atmosphere of a group of people simply by her presence. Like yeast in the dough, her love and positive influence could cause a group of people to be uplifted and encouraged.

Three-and-a-half cups of warm water:

It is the warmth of the water that activates the yeast to permeate the dough. It was the warmth of her heart and contagious smile that activated love in the lives of people around her. Like the warmth of the water, her warm heart brought out joy and peace in others.

A half cup of powdered milk:

Powdered milk is milk without the water. When mixed with warm water and yeast, the milk is restored. Time and again, the Tea Ring Lady put her arm around someone who was going through a dry time and poured an encouraging verse of scripture, like living water, into their life.

Three-fourths cup of sugar:

Knowing the Tea Ring Lady as I do, she most certainly cut back on the sugar from the original recipe. A little sugar adds just the right sweetness. The Tea Ring Lady was sweet, but not syrupy sweet. She was genuinely sweet and never for sweetness sake. Her sweetness was like the fragrance of a rose rather than the sweetness of sugar. It was the sweetness of self-giving and genuine character.

A tablespoon of salt:

Just the right amount of salt to preserve the natural flavor of the finished ring. So very often, the Tea Ring Lady, just by her presence would preserve positive outcomes in conversation and relationships. This was especially true when she was teaching children. Just by her countenance and gentle words, order would be preserved in her classroom, even when a challenging child was a potential distraction.

Four eggs:

One nutritionist said, "Whole eggs are among the most nutritious foods on earth." The Tea Ring Lady wanted her gift to be nutritious. Eggs contain nearly every known vitamin. Some of the vitamins that went into her tea rings were: Vitamin LOVE, vitamin ENCOURAGEMENT, vitamin HOPE, vitamin PEACE, vitamin WELCOME, vitamin KINDNESS, vitamin

EMPATHY. And, the egg yolks add just a touch of gold to represent the glory of the Father.

Three-fourths cup of melted butter:

Butter, in baking, serves as a shortening. That means the butter, when coating the flour, shortens the process of gluten formation creating a more tender product. The Tea Ring Lady was tender, especially with children. She could redirect a misbehaving child to take an interest in a lesson; not by demanding, but simply by speaking a tender word.

One-half cup of wheat germ:

Wheat germ is known for its nutritional value. The germ is the embryo that causes the next plant to grow. It contains the nutrients for healthy plants and for healthy bodies. Good nutrition builds healthy bodies. The Tea Ring Lady built up and never tore down. Like a tiny wheat germ, her gracious smile added a quiet bit of strength to every situation.

Twelve cups of unbleached flour:

Flour adds the largest volume of all the ingredients. Cup after cup of flour is added until just the right consistency is found. And notice, the flour is unbleached. The Tea Ring Lady was the most giving person I have ever known. Her self-giving was endless, but never for show. Her arms were always open to others with warmth and support. Her love was natural and unbleached; genuine and ordinary.

One-half cup potato flakes:

Why would she put potato flakes in a tea ring? They made the dough light and fluffy. That would please the Tea Ring Lady. She wanted to know that a bite from a tea ring would lift the spirits of the taster. Maybe it also had to do with her upbringing. She grew up on good old American garden produce, so a dash of potato would be a fitting ingredient.

Later, after shaping the dough into rings, rising a second time and baking in a hot oven, four golden-brown tea rings would sit on her cooling racks, their fragrant aroma filling the house. When it came time for them to be delivered as gifts or made ready to serve, they would be drizzled with powdered sugar frosting flavored with a touch of lemon. Well-drained maraschino cherries, carefully spaced around the sphere would add just the right amount of color, reflecting the beauty of the Tea Ring Lady herself.

"Charm is deceitful, and beauty is vain, but a woman who fears the Lord is to be praised" (Proverbs 31:30).

A NOTE FROM THE AUTHOR

Sifted through these chapters, I have appealed to the medical community and administrators of care facilities to prepare for a coming surge in the number of older people with Alzheimer's disease. I do not speak as a professional, but as a husband who cared for his wife for nearly ten years, including nine months in memory care. I am deeply appreciative of the care she was given. I write, not to criticize, but to share observations that could lead to improvements while we prepare for the future.

I asked several people to read the manuscript of this book as it was in process. Understanding my concern, one of them sent me the book, *Being Mortal,* by Atul Gawande. This quotation, in the opening pages, helps us to see the coming urgency:

> I asked Chad Boult, the geriatrics professor, what could be done to ensure that there are enough geriatricians for the surging elderly population. 'Nothing,' he said. 'It's too late.' Creating geriatric specialists takes time, and we already have far too few. In a year, fewer than three hundred doctors will complete geriatrics training in the United States, not nearly enough to replace the geriatricians going into retirement, let alone meet the needs of the next decade. [Atul Gawande, *Being Mortal* (Printed in the United States of America, address Picador, 175 Fifth Avenue, New York, N.Y., 10010) p. 52]

Dr. Gawande further reported that the strategy for the future needs to be to direct the existing geriatricians toward training all primary care doctors rather than providing care themselves.

Major problems are ahead, and the symptoms are already prevalent. It is my hope that this book will encourage leaders of the medical community to find creative solutions, such as the one Dr. Gawande suggested, to address the growing needs of people with dementia.

The Alzheimer's Association is a valuable resource for information on equipping professional caregivers. Here is a website giving useful information:

https://www.alz.org/get-involved-now/advocate/improving-care

DISCUSSION GUIDE

This discussion guide is designed to encourage conversation around the themes of *A Thief in the Pantry* by groups who are dealing with the challenges of Alzheimer's. This may include families who find themselves on a path similar to Marv and Jan's journey, as well as church groups, book clubs, care center or home health care staff and administrators, and others who have a heart for people with Alzheimer's and other dementias.

While some chapters focus on care facilities and the medical profession, other chapters describe the personal impacts of Alzheimer's on a family. It is the author's prayer that this guide will prompt practical and innovative ideas for improving the full spectrum of care for people with memory loss.

By
Marvin B. Eppard

Printable electronic version available by request from
<u>mjeppard@gmail.com</u>

Chapter 1
The Pantry

Chapter one is based on the author's memory of his grandmother's pantry. It turns into a parable of an invisible thief invading the pantry, slowly rearranging and combining items, and eventually stealing from the pantry. Throughout the parable, the cistern pump stands untouched, remaining a source of life-giving water that never runs dry.

1. What do the rearranging, combining, and stealing of pantry items represent in the parable?
2. What does the tin can by the pump represent in the parable?
3. What does the water from the pump represent in the parable?
4. In the parable, what could be done to help grandma in her confusion?
5. Does this parable apply if the grandma is not a believer in Christian faith?

Chapter 2
Alzheimer's Is Its Name

Chapter two gives the thief a name and describes things we know and don't know about it. In this chapter, we meet Jan, the central character in the story, and we learn about symptoms and characteristics of the disease.

1. Where and when did Alzheimer's disease get its name?
2. What are the early symptoms of Alzheimer's disease?
3. How long may it take for these symptoms to become apparent?
4. What are the symptoms of middle and late stages of Alzheimer's disease?
5. How does Alzheimer's impact the lives of families and friends?

Chapter 3
Shoe Boxes and Corncobs

Chapter three tells Jan's story from birth to high school graduation. Much of this comes from Jan's own writing of her life story. It is included to show the development of Jan's character and faith, and to help us see that Alzheimer's impacts real people from ordinary families.

1. How did this chapter make you feel about Jan?
2. How does this chapter help you understand the impact of Alzheimer's on an extended family?

Chapter 4
Honored and Respected

Chapter four tells of how Jan was honored by her children and respected by her peers. It illustrates the depth of her faith and helps us see the impact she made on the people around her.

1. How did Jan's relationships with family and friends equip her and her family to deal with her Alzheimer's?
2. What qualities did Jan possess that equipped her for what would come later in her life?

Chapter 5
It's Not Going Away

In chapter five the author sounds an alarm, based on Alzheimer's Association reports, about the dramatic increase in the number of people who will be dealing with this disease in the next thirty years. As the boomer generation reaches their 70's and 80's, the need for memory care will be greater than our ability to keep pace. This chapter encourages care center administrators and medical professionals to find creative ways to address the urgent needs coming in the near future.

1. How will the coming surge in the population of people in their 70's, 80's, and 90's impact the care of people with Alzheimer's and other dementias?
2. What changes could be made in the recruiting, training, and retaining of front-line day-to-day nursing staff to meet this surge?
3. What adjustments can be made by care facilities to make care safer and more efficient?
4. Since this surge may overwhelm memory care centers, what can be done to prepare and equip the general population to care for family members with Alzheimer's in their homes?

5. Alzheimer's Association studies indicate that medical professionals (primary care doctors, hospital personnel and senior care specialists, etc.) are not adequately prepared to meet the coming needs. What can be done to address these issues?

Chapter 6
Sweetcorn for Supper?

Chapter six continues the story of how Marv and Jan met, fell in love, got married, and grew together as a couple. Here we see the value of a strong marriage, built on sincere commitments, as preparation to face hardships throughout a lifetime.

1. What qualities can a couple develop early in their marriage to help them withstand the test of difficulties later in life?
2. In what ways did Jan and Marv complement each other to foster maturity in their marriage?
3. What role does Christian faith have in building an enduring marriage?

Chapter 7
This Is Alzheimer's

The purpose of chapter seven is to help the reader experience what it would be like to adjust to the needs of a family member with Alzheimer's. In this chapter, we see the early stages of this disease as we are invited into the Eppard home. It demonstrates the physical, mental, and emotional strain Alzheimer's puts on a family. This chapter tells of encounters with medical doctors both in hospitals and primary care.

1. In this chapter, the author said, "The truth is, it is a spiritual journey." What do you think he meant by this?
2. What emotions did Marv experience as the enormous scope of Jan's needs became apparent?
3. What part do you think Marv's personal vow to care for Jan as long as she lived played in his response to Jan's needs?
4. What adjustments did Marv and Jan make to prepare to face Jan's needs as she progressed through the disease?
5. Alzheimer's is a terminal disease. How did Marv grieve as he and Jan experienced more and more losses as the days, months, and years passed?
6. What is the difference between hearing your doctor say, "This is Alzheimer's," and hearing your doctor say, "This is cancer?"

Chapter 8
The Church in Action

Chapter eight begins with one of the darkest times on the journey. Instead of turning inward, Marv chose to reach out and ask for help – and the church responded.

1. What did Marv do when he came to the end of his endurance?

2. What did Marv discover through his shouting match with God?

3. Is it helpful to tell a caregiver to "be careful, the caregiver often dies before the patient?" How did Marv choose to respond to this advice?

4. How did Teresa help address the Eppard's needs? Think about how you can be a Teresa to people you know who are going through hard times.

5. Evaluate the magazine article. What happened to trigger the response from the church?

Chapter 9
Words

The conversations between Marv and Jan in chapter nine are taken directly from Marv's journal. Here he invites the reader to listen in on the words they spoke to each other as Jan moved through the middle stages of her Alzheimer's. This chapter helps us understand the challenges of communicating with a person who has significant memory loss.

1. How important is communication between a person with Alzheimer's and his or her caregivers?

2. What are some of the communication techniques a caregiver, family member, or nursing staff can use to reduce tension and accomplish goals?

3. What do you think the author meant when he said, "Communication with Jan was almost like learning a new language?"

4. Why is it important to make statements, rather than ask questions, when communicating with a person with Alzheimer's?

5. Earlier in the book (chapter 7, page 86), the author mentioned *"therapeutic lying,"* using a harmless non-truth to redirect a conversation. Is therapeutic lying a valid technique to use when communicating with an Alzheimer's patient? Is it ethical?

Chapter 10
Sprains, Shingles and Stones

Chapter ten tells the story of an especially difficult part of the Eppard's journey. An upper respiratory infection led to a premature session on hospice for Jan. A sprained knee, shingles, and kidney stones put Marv's resolve to the test. A disappointing experience with respite care turned into several months in assisted living. When a home-care agency found it impossible to meet their agreement, Marv privately employed a student nurse who made it possible for them to stay in their home for two more years.

1. Following an upper respiratory infection, the doctors seemed to have difficulty deciding if Jan should go on hospice. What did you learn from Marv and Jan's experience with hospice in this chapter?

2. The respite care provision through Medicare, which allows for a short time of relief for caregivers, is a wonderful option. How can a family be sure the facility

providing the care is adequately equipped to carry out their agreement?

3. What topics/questions should a family discuss with memory care staff/management prior to being admitted to assisted living or memory care?

4. The Eppard's experience hiring a student nurse was extremely successful. What considerations/cautions should a family keep in mind when hiring a caregiver like Kelli?

Chapter 11
Move to Memory Care

Chapter eleven tells of the painful process involved when a family can no longer care for a loved one with Alzheimer's at home and must make the move to memory care. The author sees this as the most difficult decision of the entire ten years. Eventually, Marv was able to see this transition as the best way for him to care for Jan as long as she lived.

1. What factors went into the Eppard family's decision to move Jan to memory care?

2. Circumstances such as the distance of the move, inability to set up apartments in advance, coordination with a moving company, and many others made moving day very stressful. What could be done to ease that transition?

3. What can care centers do to make the admission process into assisted living or memory care more care-oriented and less of a business transaction?

Chapter 12
A Long Cold Winter

Chapter twelve describes the difficult transition to memory care and the support of family and friends that sustained them through the long cold winter. During those months, occasional staffing shortages and stresses in relationships with staff caused some frustration. Marv expressed gratitude to the administrators and nursing staff for helping him establish a daily routine in which he was able to contribute to Jan's care. The chapter closes with the skilled assistance of hospice guiding the family through Jan's final decline.

1. Are there opportunities to expand or improve training for nurse's aides to better prepare them to work in assisted living memory care units?
2. Prior to Jan being admitted to memory care, Marv tried to clarify what his role would be in Jan's care. What can be done to better prepare a family regarding expectations while their loved one is in memory care?
3. Marv describes overhearing a loud conversation between two aides as they were helping Jan. What can be done to help the aides maintain a quiet and friendly atmosphere which reduces stress and confusion for the residents?
4. What can be done to reduce stress and foster efficiency in the care process in memory care units?
5. Recognizing that there are many differences between hospice care and assisted living memory care, are there

ways that some of the characteristics of hospice care can be incorporated into the daily care of residents in memory care?

Chapter 13
A New Road Beginning

Chapter thirteen begins with Marv and his sons and daughters gathered around Jan's bed as she took her last breath. Through a poem, Marv tells of one brief moment, about two weeks before she died, when Jan was given voice to sing and speak her final heart's desire. The chapter then gives account of what we know from the Bible about heaven and the importance of knowing Jesus as the way to the Father's house. Jan's new road is in heaven with the Savior, free from the darkness of Alzheimer's. The chapter concludes with the ultimate question, "Is your name recorded in the Book of Life?"

1. What is the most important decision a person can make in a lifetime?
2. Since the Bible is the inspired Word of God, what can we know about heaven?
3. According to God's Word in the Bible, what is the alternative to heaven?
4. What qualities did you see in Jan's life throughout the book that you would like to have in your own life?

Chapter 14
God Working For Good

In Chapter fourteen the author calls attention to the familiar verse in Romans 8:28. He then recounts the "good" things he discovered during the years of caring for Jan. The chapter ends with an awareness that the vow he had made to care for Jan as long as she lived had more facets than he had expected.

1. What good things did Marv discover he had learned during the ten years of caring for Jan?
2. What discoveries did Marv make about himself?
3. What was the source of Marv's commitment to keep going through the hard times as he cared for Jan?
4. In what ways do you experience God working "for the good of those who love him, who have been called according to his purpose?"

Chapter 15
Reflections

In this final chapter the author reflects on the focus of Jan's life. Her oft asked question, "Do you know Jesus?" was symbolic of her deep, genuine faith. Hebrews 1:1-4 became the source of assurance during the last months of Jan's life. After a final appeal to the medical and caregiving communities to always remember who they are serving, the book ends with an affirmation: "Thief *Alzheimer's* may think it was the winner in Jan's life, but that is a lie. God is victorious. His Son is the last Word."

1. What truths does Hebrews 1:1-4 teach us about Jesus that encourage us in faithful living?
2. What would be your response to Jan's question, "Do you know Jesus?"
3. Why is your response to that question so significant?

Final Overview

In this book, the author tells the love story of caring for his wife, Jan, through ten years of Alzheimer's disease as the vehicle to accomplish the following purposes: 1. To inform people of what we know and what we don't know about Alzheimer's disease. 2. To describe the impact that Alzheimer's has on a family. 3. To sound an alarm to prepare for the surge in case numbers caused by the boomer generation moving into their 70's and 80's. 4. To show the necessity of a team made up of family, community, church, and health care professionals to contribute to the care of a person with Alzheimer's. **And finally, and most importantly**, to share the good news that, like the pump in grandma's pantry, we have a source of refreshment through faith in Jesus who has sent his Holy Spirit to be a flowing stream of living water that lasts for eternity. **Alzheimer's is not the winner!**

1. Did the author accomplish his goals?
2. Which of these purposes resonates the most for you?

3. What can families, churches, communities, health care professionals, etc. do to preserve the dignity of those who suffer from severe dementia?

4. Did reading this book encourage you to gather, equip, or coach a team to share the load for a family member or friend with dementia? If so, what steps can you take to start that process?

Printed in the United States
by Baker & Taylor Publisher Services